T0294202

Praise for
From Barefoot to Bishop

"Laurent Mbanda is simply one of the most amazing and authentic Jesus followers I've had the privilege to know. It's hard to imagine a life with more dramatic or transcendent life experiences than Mbanda's. His story is an incredible journey lived on the edge of miraculous grace. We all need inspiring models to show us the way, and *From Barefoot to Bishop* captures such a model. Read it to your life-changing blessing!"

—Santiago "Jimmy" Mellado
President and CEO, Compassion International

"Laurent Mbanda's inspiring story is a testimony to what it means to be a single-minded follower of Jesus and a devoted son of Rwanda. He has persistently pursued God's divine calling wherever it led . . . out of the refugee camp to a world-class U.S. education, the executive suite of a global nonprofit, a genocide, and the heavy responsibilities of an Anglican bishop in the mountains of Rwanda. Mbanda's journey prompts all of us to dream big, fear not, and trust that God will provide."

—Dale Dawson
Founder & CEO, Bridge2Rwanda

Changing Lives Press

PO Box 140189
Howard Beach, NY 11414
www.changinglivespress.com

Library of Congress Cataloging-in-Publication Data is available through the Library of Congress.

ISBN: 978-0-9986231-0-8

Editor: Michele Matrisciani
Cover and interior design: Gary A. Rosenberg • www.thebookcouple.com

Printed in the United States of America

10   9   8   7   6   5   4   3   2   1

FROM BAREFOOT TO BISHOP

A RWANDAN REFUGEE'S JOURNEY

RT. REV. DR. LAURENT MBANDA

CHANGING LIVES PRESS

To Chantal, my lovely wife of 32 years now,
who made sure that I got what I needed
so I could keep writing, and often reminded me
of events and stories in our lives.

To my wonderful three Es: Erica, Eric, and Edwin,
for their support and encouragement,
and with thanks to Erica for quotes, comments,
and observations, which added to this story.

Contents

Acknowledgments   ix

Introduction   1

CHAPTER ONE
Turahunze—We Are Fleeing!   7

CHAPTER TWO
A Hunger for Learning   22

CHAPTER THREE
Exodus   38

CHAPTER FOUR
The Promised Land   54

CHAPTER FIVE
Plan B   72

CHAPTER SIX
God's Zigzagging Road   86

CHAPTER SEVEN
The Call to Africa   105

CHAPTER EIGHT

Into the Horror   118

CHAPTER NINE

Returning to Africa   134

CHAPTER TEN

Becoming Bishop   152

CHAPTER ELEVEN

Caring for the Children   166

EPILOGUE

Pursuing the Windows of Faith   182

About the Author   189

Photos   191

Acknowledgments

I would like to express my sincere and deep gratitude to the many friends who heard my story and encouraged me to write a book. There were even those who, over the years, offered to help write and edit it, such as Mrs. Wendy Parson and Mrs. Mary Windemuller. Thank you both!

Special thanks go to:

Tricia Crisafulli—Without your help, this book would not have been written or found its way to the publisher. You are the pumpkin!

Kelli Christiansen—Thank you for staying on the task and finding the publisher. You were fabulous.

Tom Phillips—For all the times you prayed with me and held me accountable for all we were trying to accomplish. And thank you for the book title. You inspired me, my friend.

Drayton Nabers—My ministry partner, supporter, and encourager. Thank you for checking on me as I wrote, and the willingness to offer a quiet place to reflect and write.

Chuck Welden—So many times you invited me to come to your farmhouse so I could relax and write. The offer became four-wheeler riding after a week of writing. Very much appreciated!

Chris Ordway—The challenger, you asked many questions that sparked important ideas.

Jim and Karen Weslowiski—For the times you assured me, "It will be a fantastic story." Thank you for believing in me. You also have been there for Chantal and me.

To all those who listened to my story and liked it, you inspired me to write. Thank you!

Introduction

"Take delight in the Lord, and he will give you the desires of your heart." (Psalm 37:4 NIV)

From the time I was a graduate school student, friends and colleagues would hear me talk about growing up as a Rwandan refugee in central Africa, the circumstances of my survival, how I managed to get a college education in Kenya and then pursue advanced degrees in the United States, and they'd say, "You really ought to write a book."

The story that resonated with people was not just about what happened to me. Rather, they were moved by how those things had occurred in my life—a story of faith and resilience in face of hopelessness, and a personal journey to break the cycle of poverty. This is the story I wish to tell here, through personal experiences that have shaped who I am today—from a barefoot refugee child, displaced from my home country of Rwanda to an executive with Compassion International, an international relief organization dedicated to serving the needs of impoverished children around the world, and, finally to becoming the Bishop of Shyira Diocese, covering 335 Anglican congregations in Rwanda's Northern Province.

My story begins with some of my earliest memories of Autumn 1959, the year that marked huge political and social upheaval in Rwanda. Over the next few years, more than 300,000 Tutsis were forced out of Rwanda and into neighboring countries. My family was among the refugees, and so I grew up in a series of camps and settlements in nearby Burundi, where we were poor, hungry, and ostracized. I grew up knowing what it was like to be unwanted in the country in which I lived, where opportunities for education and employment were always just beyond my grasp.

As you will read, that experience set me out on a journey—a 500-mile walk that eventually took me to Kenya in search of a college education. Along the way, I was blessed with the kindness and generosity of strangers—often people who did not have many more resources than I. Never have I forgotten these good Samaritans, without whom I would have surely lost hope and possibly my life. From Africa to the United States, where I pursued advanced degrees, I was sustained by so many people. Hearing my story and knowing my mission, they were moved to help. Many I have thanked in person; some are unknown to me, such as the anonymous donor who provided me $20,000 so I could complete my doctoral degree and begin my ministry.

As an executive with Compassion International, a U.S.-based Christian nongovernmental organization (NGO), I dedicated myself to the service of the less fortunate, especially children. My work with Compassion has taken me around the world, often seeing the best in people. Sadly, I have seen the other side, too, and in my home country. When genocide erupted in its full horror in Rwanda in April 1994—the start of 100 days of slaughter in which one million or more people were murdered and countless others were maimed, raped, and traumatized—I was sent in as part of Compassion's relief team.

Genocide is never spontaneous; it is a campaign, carefully plotted and executed. In order for those 100 days of brutal murder and mutilation to occur in 1994, there had to be practice. The massacres of 1959—and those that followed over the years, one ethnic group targeting another—started it. In his book *The Rwanda Crisis,* Gerard Prunier states that the genocide in Rwanda was the result of a process.

For centuries, three ethnic clans in Rwanda—the Tutsi, Hutu, and Twa—had lived peacefully together. But the racist poison spewed by European colonizers, who tried to make one group different from and superior to another, brought enmity to what had been coexistence and shared culture, religion, language, and origins. In 1994, a campaign of hatred, perpetrated by extremists, shattered Rwanda politically, socially, economically, and spiritually. By July 1994, the forces of the Rwandan Patriotic Front (RPF) had swept through Rwanda to end the genocide and oust the corrupt regime and the extremists responsible for the carnage. From such extreme brokenness, Rwanda has slowly rebuilt itself. Healing and reconciliation after such unspeakable brutality, neighbor against neighbor, has been a long process that continues to this day.

As a former refugee, my work with Compassion to bring relief to Rwanda during and immediately after the genocide was an emotional homecoming. As a small child, I had to leave Rwanda, but Rwanda had never left me. Helping my home country rebuild and advocating for the children who lived there took me back to my roots and to my past. I know what it's like to live in fear and deprivation, to escape death, and to pray for a better life. These experiences shaped me profoundly and ultimately led me to become Bishop of Shyira Diocese.

My call to leadership has put me at the pulpit of the cathedral in Musanze, Rwanda's second-largest city and the hub of the Northern Province, and in rural parishes to meet, encourage, and counsel our pastors. I also have taken on a highly personal mission: to tend to God's vulnerable children—poor, undernourished, and in need of education and spiritual direction. Establishing preschools for these rural Rwandan children, to give thousands of unattended children a place to go while their mothers work the fields, tote water, and gather firewood, was my first act as bishop. These children are not neglected. Their mothers must work each day in order for the family to have food and drinking water. The distended bellies of those who do not get enough to eat or the right kinds of food cause an ache in my own stomach, because I know what it's like. I remember. I was one of those children fifty-five years ago.

Someone recently asked me what it felt like to have gone from extreme poverty and hunger to being supported by others, sometimes in the most surprising ways. I can say that all of it—the good and the bad—has helped me grow and become a better person, capable of love and compassion. Having known deprivation, I am sensitive to the needs of others, especially children who live with poverty, hunger, and disease. According to the United Nations Millennium Development Project, six million children under the age of five die from malnutrition every year. More than 800 million people go to bed hungry every day; 300 million of them are children.

Poverty, hunger, and malnutrition continue to be pandemics. The U.N. Food and Agriculture Organization has estimated that 239 million people in sub-Saharan Africa were hungry or undernourished in 2010 (the most recent estimate), while 925 million people worldwide were hungry.* The principal cause of hunger is poverty, which is often exacerbated by conflict and prolonged drought.

For me, these numbers are more than dire statistics. They echo the story of my life, not only my early experiences but also throughout my career in ministry and humanitarian service. For nearly two decades, I worked in the field, covering Africa, Asia, and Latin America, and as an executive for Compassion International, based in Colorado Springs. With Compassion International, I found a home and a meaningful career providing resources and support to help the most vulnerable of those in need: the children. I am proud to have served as vice chairman on the global board of Compassion International, as a chairman of Food for the Hungry Associates, and on the global board of Opportunity International, all which are dedicated to serving the poor, the hungry, and the vulnerable, especially in developing nations. In addition, over the years, I have served on a good number of international and local boards. Through these organizations, as well as in my role as Bishop of Shyira Diocese in Rwanda, I continue to pursue a life of meaning and purpose, which is my way of giving thanks and giving back.

Mine is a story of faith, a personal expression of my religious beliefs and spiritual life. My hope is that regardless of

*Food and Agriculture Organization of the United Nations, "The State of Food Insecurity in the World," 2010. http://www.fao.org/docrep/013/i1683e/i1683e.pdf

whether you see yourself as a person of faith, you will gain the understanding that all of us are shaped by the circumstances of our lives, especially the challenges we face, and by the people who touch us and who we touch along the way.

When we really pay attention and look back on our lives, we see that we do not journey by ourselves. Even in the midst of the most brutal challenges, dire problems, or bitter disappointments, we are not alone. There are people who step forward to help or to console. My journey is living proof of that. And, I believe, we are never alone spiritually, and that God, who loves us, will never abandon us and showers us with grace.

If I could condense all these pages into one word, it would be hope. No matter where we are, where we've come from, or what we face, there is hope. And the most profound joy in life is to be that hope for others.

Rt. Rev. Laurent Mbanda, Ph.D.
Musanze, Rwanda • Spring 2017

CHAPTER ONE

Turahunze—
We Are Fleeing!

*"Ask and it will be given to you; seek and you will
find; knock and the door will be opened to you."*
(*Matthew 7:7 NIV*)

November 1959

The air was full of smoke. All around us, huts and houses
were burning, their thatched roofs lighting up like
torches. The screams and shouts and the smoke that stung
my eyes and nose told me something was very wrong. But I
didn't know what and I didn't know why. A month after my
fifth birthday, all my mind knew was that there was danger,
and I was terrified.

I was born in the community of Nshili in southern Rwanda.
Like many rural Rwandans, my family had about five acres
of land for growing food, and my grandparents, who lived
nearby, had a banana grove. The houses were made of mud
brick, formed from the red-brown earth and dried in the sun.
Most had thatched roofs, but our house had tile roofing made
from clay hardened by fire.

My father was a teacher and had just left for the village school where he taught. Although he only finished Grade 6, he had been trained for a year in pedagogy and was one of the best students in the teacher-training program. He was a natural-born teacher. I was at home with my mother, who was expecting her fourth child. When we smelled the smoke and heard the shouts and screams, we ran outside to find people streaming down the hillsides, fleeing their burning homes. Chasing behind them were people yelling and waving torches, wearing shabby clothes and headdresses made of banana leaves—frightening costumes, especially to a small child. I clung to my mother's skirt, too frightened to make a sound. Through the fabric, I could feel her trembling.

She grabbed my hand. We ran to my grandparents' home and hid among the banana trees. The smoke grew thicker as more houses were set ablaze, but ours was saved because of the tiled roof.

When this angry militia finally passed, the adults regrouped. My grandfather was with the other men, talking about what had happened and what we should do. I stayed with my mother, but kept looking around for my father.

"Where's Daddy?" I asked my mother.

"At school," she said, in a tone that did not invite any more questions.

Although I was too young to know it then, her reply was more hope than fact. The truth was, we didn't know where my father was or even if he was still alive. Because my father was a teacher, he had a bit of status in this small village, although we were humble like everyone else. But that, and the fact that he was from a certain ethnic clan, made him a target. If that mob in shabby clothes and banana leaves found him, my father would be dead.

In my village of Nshili, we never went hungry. Our gardens and fields provided what we needed to eat and be healthy. All around us was bush and forest, where people hunted for meat. But after the invasion of that mob and the burning of the houses, we could no longer stay. *"Turahunze!"* The word spread like a breath of wind. *"Turahunze!* We are fleeing!" We were headed to Burundi, a neighboring country, a walk to the border of about 15 to 20 kilometers (9 to 12 miles).

About twenty families, roughly one hundred people, left that night. It was pitch black, the sky heavy with clouds because it was the rainy season. We could hear each other walking and the muffled breaths of people around us, but we couldn't see each other. A group of men went ahead, carrying bows and arrows and spears. They were followed by women and children, toting what little they could. The smallest children were carried. Those who were old enough and big enough, like me, were held by the hand. Another group of armed men followed. The darkness was our protection.

"Shh-shh. Keep quiet. Go slow!" people whispered to one another, especially to the children.

Noise was dangerous; it could get us killed. But it was nearly impossible for so many people to move quietly in the dark through the heavy overgrowth of bushes and trees. With every step, a twig snapped, a branch rustled. We moved and stopped, straining in the silence to discern the sounds. Was something there? Were we being followed?

After a few hours, there were other sounds: the whispers and whimpers of children. "I'm tired." "I'm hungry."

My arm was tired from being held by the hand and led along. Mother was nine months into her pregnancy, so walking for her was difficult. In her fear for her children, her missing husband, and herself, my mother gripped me tightly and would not be letting go. When my legs could no longer carry me, my paternal uncle picked me up and put me on his shoulders. I clung to him, my head bobbing with sleepiness, all the while wishing that my father was the one carrying me.

It took most of the night to make our slow progress—walking and waiting, walking and waiting. Finally, we crossed the border into Burundi and reached the first refugee receiving center. I have no memories of that first night in the center, but the next day I was with my grandmother. All day I kept asking for my mother. Finally, my paternal grandmother called me aside and told me not to worry. "We're going to see her," she promised.

I walked with her to a Danish Baptist church and mission center, which had a small, makeshift hospital. My mother was there, with my new baby brother.

A nurse at the hospital, a Burundi man, offered to take my family to his house to live. My family gladly accepted the offer. There were five of us: my mother; my sisters, Odette and Speciose, ages three and two, respectively; my newborn baby brother, Claude; and myself. (Later, my grandfather's family of five spent a few days there.) Although this man and his family did not have much to share and frequently we would not have enough to eat, we never forgot his generosity. The refugee center was soon overwhelmed by the number of Rwandans who were fleeing the country. Hungry and in need of shelter, Rwandan refugees went into the villages nearby, looking for food and asking for a place to stay.

About four hours away by foot was the Anglican Church mission station at Buye, which people said was better equipped to handle refugees. Buye had food supplies, first aid, even small clinics to handle the refugees, and it also offered temporary huts to shelter families, After a few weeks, when my mother could make the trip, we went there. I never stopped thinking about my father, wondering where he was and how he would find us. But I knew better than to keep asking. No one had any answers. We had heard stories that my father had been hidden by one of the priests at the Catholic mission station at Cyahinda, a day's walk from our home village of Nshili. We hoped and prayed that this was true.

The refugee center at Buye was more organized. Workers from the United Nations High Commissioner for Refugees and the Red Cross documented every person who entered the center. As we waited our turn to be officially received, we could see there was food. My eyes followed a long line of children holding blue cups, who waited for a portion of powdered milk mixed with water.

Hunger ate at my empty stomach. It had been almost two days since I had something to eat. Every time I watched one of the children walk away with one of those cups of milk to share a sip with other family members, I could taste it. I could not wait until it was my turn. Standing in that line, which might have held as many as thirty children but looked to be endless, my knees started to buckle. I wanted to sit down, but if I did, I would never make it to the front of that line. I wanted to push someone, to make them go faster, but the line moved so slowly. As I got nearer to the front, I craned my neck to see if there was any milk left. What if they ran out before I got there? I looked back toward my mother, who waited on the side with the adults in my family. She waved me on with her hand, telling me to just keep moving forward.

Dizzy from hunger and heat, exhausted physically and emotionally, I managed one step at a time. Another child ran past me, carrying one of those precious blue cups. If only I could take a small sip.

Finally I was near the front. I held a blue cup in my hand and watched as the people dispensing the milk ladled it out to the children ahead of me. I watched that liquid pour in, imagining the taste of it in my mouth and filling my empty stomach.

Then it was my turn. I held out my cup, waiting for it to be filled.

Suddenly, I was lifted off my feet by a pair of strong arms. I kicked and yelled, struggling to get free. "I want my milk! I want my milk!" If I lost my place in line, there would be nothing for me.

"Where is your mother?" the man cried.

It was my father! He had been one of the volunteers serving the children. Looking back, it is no surprise that's where we finally met him. My father dedicated his life to children as a teacher; advocacy for the littlest ones was a legacy I would inherit from him. But as I held onto him that day at Buye and cried, it was because all I wanted was my milk.

I never got any. Instead my father carried me in the other direction, to my mother and a joyful reunion with the family. To this day, when this story is told, I'm teased about being "the boy who would have traded his father for a cup of milk."

My father had hidden in the Catholic mission center until the worst of the danger was over. Then he crossed the border into Burundi, looking for us. It was a small miracle that we met up with him in Buye because there were so many displaced people spread across numerous refugee camps.

From the feeding center, we were moved into one of the huts that had been built at Buye for the refugees. People from the same villages were grouped together, so that every day we saw our friends and neighbors. Home was all anyone talked about; going home was all they wanted to do.

"When this cools down, we'll go back," I heard people say, as I walked around up and down a row of huts in the refugee settlement.

The same message was echoed by Burundi authorities who came to address the refugees: "When peace returns, you will go back to your country."

From Buye, a few of the refugees started going back to Rwanda, especially those who lived near the border. Some had left cows and other animals behind; others wanted to know if their houses were still standing. Sometimes they went back to get their families, believing things had quieted down and they were safe.

After nearly five months in the refugee camp, some Catholic priests who were friends of my father came to take him back to Rwanda. They told him it was peaceful again and urged my father to repatriate our family. My father left to see for himself and, after a few weeks, he came back for us. We moved back to Rwanda, along with many eager others. But in early 1960, violence erupted again. Millions of Rwandan refugees fled the country—to Burundi, Uganda, Tanzania, and later to Kenya, Europe, or even the United States. My family, as a family, fled for a second and final time back to the Anglican mission and refugee center at Buye.

Soon after our return to the refugee camp, my father's skills as a teacher were needed by an Anglican missionary and a British medical doctor at another camp called Kayongozi. My father agreed to go and provide schooling for the refugee children there, so we, along with about one hundred other people, were loaded onto a convoy of large canvas-covered trucks. My father and several other men stood in the back of those trucks, reaching down, gripping the forearms of men and women, and hoisting them up, one by one. The children were buoyed and brigaded to the arms of their families, who had somehow stashed their few belongings to make room for everyone.

It seemed so much better this time, riding in a truck instead of walking across the border or making our way to Buye. But the roads were not good and it was the rainy season. Despite the "turn boy" who was assigned to adjust the canvas on top of the trucks to keep us from getting soaked, the rain managed to detain us. The truck frequently got stuck in deep trenches of mud, and the men had to get out and push as the back tires spun, skidding us aimlessly. The smell of the diesel fuel and the thick exhaust, along with the pitch and roll of the truck along the rutted roads, made people sick. One person vomited and then another; soon nearly everyone was ill. We continued in this way for a day and a half, until we finally reached Kayongozi.

As we approached the camp, people began storming our truck. Many had not seen family members or friends for months. Some had lost children along the way. In the panic and danger, running away in the night, it was so easy to slip and fall, to lose grip on a hand, to get lost in the chaos.

"What are they doing?" I asked my father. The voices were getting louder and more desperate sounding.

"They want to know who we are and where we've come from," he explained. "They are all looking for someone."

I remembered how tightly I had been held and began to understand the hope these people might have been clinging to as our truck began letting off more refugees. From that day on, whenever a truck arrived at the refugee settlement, it was also reason to hope that someone who was lost or missing would finally be found. Sometimes there were joyful reunions; other times only disappointment.

At Kayongozi, we recognized people from our village, which gave us a sense of security and belonging. Here, so far away from home, were people—friends—who recognized us. But we were there only a few weeks. They had enough teachers already, so there was no room for my father at the school. We had to move again, this time deeper into Burundi, near the Tanzanian border, to a new camp called Kigamba where my father's skills as a teacher were needed. My grandparents, my uncles and aunts, and the rest of the extended family decided to stay at Kayongozi which had good supplies and facilities for receiving refugees. So my parents, siblings, and I went alone.

Kigamba was a new camp, with a lack of infrastructure to handle the overflow of refugees. The huts were so tiny that an adult could not lie on the ground without his feet sticking out the open door. Heavily forested, the area was home to many wild animals, including lions and hyenas. Every night, huge fires were built around the camp to keep the animals away, and men would take turns staying awake to keep watch. I used to huddle with them around that fire until I grew sleepy. It seemed so much safer than staying in a tiny hut with no door.

At night, as darkness blanketed the camp, the roar of the lions and the cry of the hyenas haunted me. But the most frightening sounds of all were the screams and shouts of people warning us that lions and hyenas had come into the camp to get at the goats. Sometimes these animals killed people, too.

"They're coming! They're coming!" they'd shout.

While the children hid inside the huts, the adults stood outside and banged on metal jerry cans to frighten the predators away.

I buried my head to keep from hearing anymore.

There hadn't been a school at Kigamba until my father started one. Within days of our arrival, he began teaching outdoors, literally under the trees. As word spread, children began to gather, sitting on the ground, using sticks and dirt to write and count.

When it rained, there was no school. If someone saw a snake—which often was just a stick on the ground—students would run home in the middle of a lesson. But somehow my father made it work. He urged parents to bring their children to the new school and also used the structure of the camp to spread the word. Whenever food and other supplies were distributed, camp organizers announced the school was open and needed teachers and helpers. The qualifications for teachers were simple: You had to be able to read and write, and you had to be taller than the students. By the time I reached Grade 3, at around nine or ten years old, I started tutoring the younger students.

More permanent housing was being built and we were moved into circular houses made of mud and logs, topped by a thatch roof that allowed smoke from the fire inside to escape. Some of the huts also had small openings cut into the sides for ventilation. The huts had one room with a divider between where the adults and the children slept on thin mats. People began to lose hope of ever going back to Rwanda. Others, including my father, were more accepting of the situation and agreed that we needed to continue to build.

By the time I reached Grade 5, the High Commissioner for Refugees (UNHCR) had built a school and turned it over to the Burundi government, which started recruiting certified teachers. It was then that my qualified but undertrained father lost his job. When the government-operated school turned out to be too far for the youngest students to walk to every day, my father started a primary school at the camp for the youngest children and those in the earliest grades.

On Sundays, he held worship services at the school for the people in the community. Later, when the World Gospel Mission sent lay preachers (i.e., unordained ministers) to the camp, my father continued as part of the team. I had been growing in faith, thanks to the teaching of the missionaries who served our refugee camp. These missionaries had worked particularly hard to convert my father, who had been raised Catholic. Eventually, my father became an evangelical Christian, which meant giving up drinking and smoking, both of which he enjoyed. At first, my mother was skeptical. She, too, drank the homebrew she made and enjoyed her tobacco in a pipe. After my father remained faithful to his new church tradition for a year, and even became a lay preacher, my mother converted, too. I was about seven years old when we children followed our parents and became evangelical Christians. I proudly accompanied my father to church each Sunday, carrying his books and his Bible, and sometimes bringing along chairs and benches for those who attended services.

Many devout Christians remember the day of their conversion, that moment when they "received Christ" and claimed him as their personal savior. For me, though, there is no such memory of a special day. Receiving Christ was a weekly event for me. The missionaries who came to our camp would bring small Bible storybooks with pictures in them as well as crayons, candies, and even used clothing. Whenever they invited someone to come forward and be claimed as one of Christ's own, down the aisle I went—every week! I wanted those little gifts! I made a commitment.

My father planted fruit trees and banana trees, which he obtained from a nearby mission center, so that we would be able to feed ourselves in the future. Other refugees became very angry with him, saying it was a bad precedent. To put down roots in such a place was to give up our home in Rwanda—and any hope of going back to our homeland.

Soon a brutal reality set in. After three years of feeding us, the Red Cross and World Food Program began weaning the refugees off humanitarian aid. The intention was to get people to become more self-sufficient, but most people were not prepared to fend for themselves. Even those who had planted gardens had little for themselves or to share, because wild pigs often came out of the jungle at night and ate everything. People began to die of starvation. Poor hygiene in some of the huts led to cholera and dysentery. The death toll mounted over three months—easily hundreds of people out of a camp population of about eleven thousand.

Aid trucks with food came only a few times a week. We children followed along behind them, picking up beans that fell off the truck backs. A handful of boiled and mashed beans could be watered down into a thin porridge a satisfying meal in itself.

To get food, people ventured into surrounding villages, but they were considered unwelcome interlopers. We did not speak exactly the same language, even though Kirundi, Burundi's language, and my native language Kinyarwanda are similar. The refugees and the Burundi villagers kept themselves separate; each group regarded the other as strangers.

As hunger and starvation worsened, people tried to leave Kigamba. Some returned to the Kayangoza camp; others moved to Uganda and Tanzania and later to Mushiha, another new camp, about 25 kilometers (roughly 15 miles) from Kigamba and even closer to the Tanzanian border. The Burundi government tried to contain the refugees by putting up roadblocks, so that displaced people wouldn't wander the countryside or venture into towns and villages, causing problems, becoming drunk on local "homebrew," or even committing crimes.

Kigamba had become our home, so we stayed there. But many nights we went to bed without food. My hair turned reddish and my stomach swelled, sure signs of malnutrition. To keep us alive, my father began to strategically place my siblings with other relatives. My baby brother, Claude, who was about four years old, was sent to live with my grandparents in Kayongoza, where there was more secure food supplies. My younger sister, Speciose, went to live with family members in a camp called Muramba, where she stayed for almost six years. My other younger sister, Odette, and I remained with our parents.

As the oldest, I took it upon myself to find food. Soon, it became a full-time activity, more important than school. My sister and I scrounged in the forest, looking for wild fruit (*amanazi,* which was also a favorite of the monkeys) and bringing back what little we could find. Often, our hands were empty. I tried to be brave. I learned to cry silently and to not ask my mother for something to eat because I knew how painful it was for her to tell me there was nothing. We moved more slowly to conserve our energy. When we sat down, we did not get up too fast so as to not become lightheaded.

One day there was nothing to eat—nothing at all. I remember it so clearly. I was eleven years old, tall for my age (I am six foot five now) and had the appetite of a growing boy. I could not believe that we would starve. Surely God, who led the Israelites through the desert, who provided manna every morning for Moses and his people, would give us food, too. I believed it so strongly; I knew it had to be true.

"Boil water," I told my mother that day, "because God is going to provide for us."

Her only response was to laugh, because what I had said was so ridiculous.

But I refused to be discouraged and wandered behind the house and into the forest.

I stumbled along, faint from hunger, yet confident that I would not go back to my mother empty-handed. My hunger was great, but my faith was greater. The Lord would provide, I told myself over and over while searching for food.

And there, under a tree, was a pumpkin—a perfect, round, orange pumpkin.

What was it doing there? Could it be a trap to capture animals? Maybe it was poisoned.

I checked over every inch of that thick rind but couldn't find a scratch or a nick where poison could have contaminated it. Then I tried to find the vine from which it grew, but there was nothing—no vine, no leaves, no roots. This frightened me, because it seemed a real possibility that someone was trying to poison some poor Rwandan refugee wandering in the forest looking for food. But the pumpkin looked so perfect. The only explanation was that it was, truly, a gift from God.

Looking around, I tried to see if someone had been walking through the forest and dropped it, but there was no one in sight and no trace of footprints. I picked up that pumpkin and ran home.

"Here!" I called out to my mother. "I found this."

She couldn't believe her eyes. "Where did you get this?"

"In the forest."

My mother picked up that pumpkin. "Someone is targeting us," she said. "They are trying to poison us—to get rid of us."

She turned the pumpkin over and over, just as I had, looking at the rind for some scratch or mark, something that would indicate there was something wrong with it. Finding nothing, we took a leap of faith. My mother boiled water, just as I had told her to that morning, and she cooked that pumpkin. I ate with joy as every bite went into my mouth and filled my stomach. No matter how delicious, no meal since then can compare with that bowl of cooked pumpkin. It was a true celebration, knowing we would live.

That night, my belly full, I knew what had happened. I had put my trust in God that He would provide. It was a lesson of faith that would stay with me the rest of my life.

CHAPTER TWO

A Hunger for Learning

*"Trust in the Lord with all your heart and lean not on
your own understanding." (Proverbs 3:5 NIV)*

When I was about nine years old, my schooling was disrupted by a sad reality: My father did not earn enough money to support our family. Sometimes, I resented my father for paying so much attention to his students while not focusing enough on whether his own children had enough to eat. We all had to pitch in—even if that meant missing classes. For my part, I went into "business," skipping school to go into nearby village centers to sell cigarettes (always singly, since no one could afford a pack), along with Bic pens, pencils, and candies. My mother grew crops in her garden and hired herself out to Burundi people near the camp to tend their gardens. She also made pastries, called *amandazi,* which looked like doughnuts. I sold them at school and on market days when people came to town to sell their produce and goods.

My father recognized what I was doing for the family and made a contribution to my business: his old bicycle—a *pneu ballon* (a fat-tire bicycle). I rode that bicycle to school and back and used it to carry goods to trade and sell. Because my father could not miss school, when we had some money, I accompanied my mother when she traveled the 25 kilometers (15.5 miles) to the market to buy food. I would help carry whatever she bought, and the more money we had, the more we could buy. As I got older, I made more frequent trips and ventured farther from the refugee camp to sell my goods. By the time I was eleven years old and in Grade 5, I attended school only three or four days out of six each week.

Even though I performed well academically and kept advancing to the next grade on schedule, many of my teachers derided me for being absent so much. "You will never amount to anything," one teacher sneered. Another, convinced I wasn't serious about my studies, told me to "leave school and go do business instead!" Their words crushed me because it was clear that they saw me, a schoolmaster's son, as not valuing learning, which was hardly the truth. I wanted an education more than anything.

For many years, my family's only food was what we managed to grow or scrounge in the jungle. During my father's services of worship, we prayed to God and learned that the Israelites received the message the Lord gave Moses: "I will rain down bread from heaven for you. The people are to go out each day and gather enough for that day" (Exodus 16 NIV).

So that's what we did. Often our refugee community would look for *amanazi,* a fruit that would fall from the trees in the jungle. *Amanazi* was our manna: bread from heaven. Hundreds of children and even adults would go out every morning to collect *amanazi.* The teachers at the government-sanctioned schools and the nurses, agronomists, and government officials who visited the refugee camp looked like they had enough to eat; they didn't need to pray for crumbs to drop from heaven. While we had hardly the clothes on our backs and few blankets, our visitors had modest and clean clothes. I did not envy them as much as I studied them, and I decided that, one day, I would live as they did.

I vowed that when that day came, my family and I would have more than a one-room hut to live in. Never again would we have to worry about having enough to eat. When that day came, I would be able to afford a bicycle, then a motorcycle. My fascination with motorcycles started when I was a young child in Burundi. The first time I saw a man riding with his shirt open, the wind making a bubble out of the back of it, I thought that was something. I saw the priests at the Catholic mission riding them too. At the refugee camp, two men who worked for a nongovernment organization (NGO) always arrived on a Suzuki 125 and a Honda 175.

Motorcycles and houses would have to wait. As I spun dreams about a prosperous future for myself and my family, I quickly realized that nothing could be accomplished without an education. Even as good as I was at doing business, I could not turn my back on my first role model regarding learning: my father. He had shown me that even without chairs, desks, notebooks, pencils, or books, one could still gain knowledge and a life's purpose, if he wanted it. Fortunately, some of my teachers understood my predicament and helped me realize that taking care of my family didn't have to exclude an education. They encouraged me to keep up my studies while working to support my family. I remember one day when a teacher called me aside. "You are a smart young man with a bright future," he said kindly. "You work very hard." Hearing his words, I wondered if he meant in school or in business. Now, I realize he probably meant both. This teacher encouraged me to get notes from my classmates and to keep studying on my own. "If you need help," he said, "come see me."

This teacher and a few others made a point to reach out to me, encouraging me to see that it was possible to help provide for my family and also to continue with school. Even when other teachers ridiculed for me for missing so much school and not applying myself, I never thought of quitting.

By the time I was thirteen years old, my business had expanded, and so had my education to Grade 7. I was selling home-brewed alcohol that my mother made from sorghum, a cereal grain that grows tall like corn and can be used for flour, for porridge, or for brewing. I would also go to the local Burundi brewery, *Dépôt Brarudi,* to buy a case of twelve bottles of Primus beer (two cases when I had the money) and then I would sell them to thirsty travelers at the Burundi–Tanzania border. Being a beer vendor was a good business, and my monthly income increased to the point that I was earning more than my teachers (I was making the equivalent of $50 per month). When some of my teachers figured out that I had more money than they did, they were less eager to help me with my missed schoolwork. But there were always some who helped me and who I, in turn, befriended. When I had a little extra money, I would sometimes buy them small gifts to show my appreciation.

Anyone looking at me in those days—selling beer and cigarettes, hawking pens and pencils in the market—likely would have said, "That young man will be a merchant one day." Indeed, I can certainly look back and see the roots of my passion for social entrepreneurship. As much as business appealed to me, though, I had another calling: ministry.

From the time my family had become Evangelical Christians, my dream had been to attend high school and then

Bible college. Fulfilling that dream meant I had to overcome the challenge that confronted all Rwandan refugees: the pervasive bias against us in the Burundi school system.

Burundi did not have enough secondary (high) schools (Grades 8–12) to accommodate all students. Therefore, the Burundi government's policy was to make Burundi students the priority while setting a strict quota on the number of refugees admitted to secondary school. In order to be considered for admission, refugee students had to do more than just pass the national qualifying exam; we had to do exceptionally well in order to earn one of the few slots allocated for us.

My dual life of squeezing in school while earning money for my family caught up with me. By the time I was fourteen, I had taken the national exam twice, repeating Grade 7 in the process, but I did not achieve a score that would allow me to be admitted into high school. Instead of becoming discouraged and blaming the Burundi government's policies against refugees, I became even more motivated. I was never giving up on my dream!

But I did have to accept the reality of the situation—that I was an outsider, a Rwandan living in Burundi. In my trading and selling business, I tried to blend in and disguise my true identity, masking my accent and intonation. But when it came to getting an education, there was no hiding my refugee status. If the Burundi government-run schools didn't want me, then I would have to go someplace where I was accepted. However, my immediate concern was how to get to Grade 8.

My father's missionary friend, Mr. Kirkpatrick, stopped me after church services one day. "Laurent," he asked, "what are your plans?"

It was the first time someone outside my immediate family had asked me such a question. Mr. Kirkpatrick was a close friend to my father and had taken interest in me, so I could tell by the way Mr. Kirkpatrick asked that this was more than a polite inquiry or a way to strike up a conversation. "I want to go to secondary school," I told him. "My dream is to attend one that prepares young people for Christian ministry."

Mr. Kirkpatrick nodded as I spoke. Being a missionary, he was pleased that I was drawn to a vocation in ministry and was dedicated to pursuing it. "There is one problem," I added, no longer sounding as optimistic and confident as I had a minute before. "I cannot get into secondary school. I didn't score high enough on the national exam."

The well-known education policies and quotas for Rwandan refugees were stacked against me, and my working at the same time as attending school made my odds even worse. Despite those things, Mr. Kirkpatrick urged me to continue to have faith. Keep pursuing your plans, and don't give up," he said to me steadily. "Above all, pray."

I was not to take the national examination a third time, so I could only pursue an alternative education. While Mr. Kirkpatrick looked into the possibilities for me, my father asked about vocational schools, even though that was not what I wanted. Without knowing how this would be resolved, I could only have faith and keep praying.

My prayers were soon answered when, thanks to Mr. Kirkpatrick's contacts, I was invited to see one of the other missionaries and a local pastor at the World Gospel mission station that provided leadership for the church in our camp. I was to interview with them in the hope of being recommended for school. Since I had good grades, I did qualify as a student. The interview went well as I answered their questions about my faith and scripture and where I felt God was leading me. As I departed, they told me to get ready to go to

Mweya Bible School, a boarding school located in the province of Gitega in central Burundi.

I couldn't wait to get home and tell my parents. There was just one problem: The school was 150 kilometers (93 miles) from the camp and I had no money for a transport ticket. My parents, however, were determined to provide this opportunity for me. They borrowed the money from a friend to buy a ticket, gave me a little money for the basics I needed, and sent me off—a sixteen-year-old leaving my parents for the first time.

I was so excited at the opportunity to continue my education, especially at a boarding school away from the refugee camp. I had seen other kids from the camp go away to boarding schools and noticed how much better they looked when they returned to visit. While I was nervous about what was ahead, I was elated that my path was continuing. With my parents' encouragement and knowing my siblings were in good hands, I had no fear for them as I left.

I walked 25 kilometers (15.5 miles) to the town of Cankuzo, wearing my rubber flip-flops, the only footwear I had. Most of the time, I went barefoot because shoes were a luxury. As I passed through the villages along the way, Rwandan refugees would notice my bags and ask where I was going and why. They were used to seeing students my age going off to boarding schools, but I had left later in the term than others. Therefore, they probably wondered where I was going. When they found out I was going to school, some of them reached into their pockets and handed me a few francs, saying something like "My child, buy yourself a banana or a drink on the way." Looking back, that kind of generosity and solidarity among the Rwandan refugees still moves me. Unfortunately, it has been lost somehow.

The journey to Cankuzo took me several hours over rough roads until I finally reached the center of this small town. There, I met up with a store owner who, I had been told, had an old Toyota Stout pickup truck, which he used to take passengers to Gitega. I spent the night outside that storefront, lying on the ground with my bag as a pillow, under the watchful eye of men patrolling the stores. Then, early the next day, the truck was loaded with passengers and we left for Gitega. Most were dropped off at destinations along the way and others got on. By the time we reached Gitega, we were still a full load crammed into the back.

I did not know what would await me, how I would be received by others, what the school would be like, or even how I would compare to the other students. I had heard of students who had failed out of boarding school and could not continue their secondary education. The system, I knew, was not designed to encourage students to continue; rather it seemed set up to eliminate them. Committing to working as hard as I could, I vowed I would not be one of those sent back.

I arrived around noon at Gitega, the second-largest city in Burundi after the capital, Bujumbura, and a commercial center. Here, for the first time, I saw paved roads, beautiful houses painted in vibrant colors, numerous stores, and sturdy fences with big gates at the entrance of houses. Coming from rural village areas and, more specifically, from the refugee resettlement with mud houses and grass-thatched roofs, I was amazed by what I saw that I didn't even know existed. I wished that someday I could step into one of those houses.

Most of the schools were clustered around the town of Gitega. There was also a large military barracks, well known for its military training and discipline and for being home to tough commandos, as well as an old prison, and a colonial-era building that housed the governor of Gitega's office. Small shops in a row like a street mall bordered a large open market in the center of the city.

In the 1970s, Gitega was a modern city. The size of the city and the buildings, the diverse crowds of well-dressed Arab and African people, and the amount of cars on the streets were a real eye-opener for a young man like me. I heard Swahili being spoken everywhere and only understood a few words. The city was intimidating—a busy place full of pickpockets—and I was glad I had a destination and didn't have to wander about looking for shelter. Without even stopping to get something to eat, I left the bustling city center and set out to walk another 18 kilometers (11 miles) to Mweya, where I arrived in the evening that same day. I was so excited to have finally arrived there that I nearly ran when the mission station came into sight. Set on a hill, its lights illuminated the crest, recalling the words in Matthew: "A town built on a hill cannot be hidden" (Matthew 5:14 NIV). Until this time, I had only seen small mission stations with small lights. Walking up the entrance road bordered by eucalyptus and cedar trees, I knew I was entering a special place but also one that was intimidating. Once inside the well-lit compound, I could see it was spotless with a beautiful chapel, the large Mweya Bible School, and, beyond them, a basketball court and a soccer field. Security watchmen with walkie-talkies and flashlights passed; I nodded respectfully and kept walking.

At the administration office, I was welcomed as a new boarding student. While my admission to the school had been arranged, my tuition had not been. I knew I would have to come up with some money, but it was more than what I had with me. If I wanted to stay there and study, I would need to work.

During my first week, I heard from some of the other

students that they sometimes got odd jobs on the weekends. I set out to ask around the mission station about what jobs I could perform. I met Mr. and Mrs. Bernie MacLean, who were American missionaries; Mr. MacLean also was in charge of the printing operation at the mission station. "Do you have a job for me? I need to earn money for school," I explained in French. In addition to speaking Kinyarwanda, Rwandan students were taught French, the official language, in Burundi.

Mrs. MacLean took one look at me—a sixteen-year-old, well over six feet tall (and soon to reach my full height of six feet five inches)—and said she'd give me a job on Saturdays. My first task was to cut grass by hand using a *coup-coup*, a tool with a curved blade sharpened on both sides. It was a hot and tiring job but one I did eagerly because it paid for my schooling. By the next quarter, I had apparently proved myself to be honest and reliable enough for more jobs around the MacLean house grounds. They respected me for being hard-working, and I passed their test for honesty and integrity when they left a few coins here and there to see if I would take them, which I never did. When Mrs. MacLean brought me to work inside their house, where I washed dishes and mopped floors, I knew I had earned their trust.

As much as I appreciated this opportunity and needed the wages, I hated being a house servant, mostly because of my low status among the other boys at school. These boys were Burundi citizens, not refugees like me. Though most were not wealthy, their families had more resources than mine. For them, tuition was not a problem, and some had scholarships or had been pledged assistance by their home church missions. Those few who did work only wanted to earn extra spending money. And some came from well-to-do families who had everything they wanted.

"Did you come here for school or to do housework?" some of them would ask me. They even tried to shame me, asking what the people of my village would think if they knew the kind of work I was doing. There weren't many girls around the school, and I felt shy around them, especially when they would ask me questions with little smiles. "So are you done working?" they'd ask before turning their heads and giggling; I knew they were laughing at me.

No matter how some of the other students treated me, I was grateful to work for the MacLeans. It didn't matter if others looked down on me: I knew why I did the "housework" others disdained. Without that work, I could not pay my tuition or buy any personal items. When I managed to save some extra money, I sent it home to my parents.

Working for the MacLeans, I began picking up a few English words and basic phrases: *Here clean? More. Thank you. Bye-bye. Saturday come back?* I learned the names of food items and kitchen utensils. I studied the map of the United States and could pick out Indiana, where the MacLeans' home mission was based. I learned the names of several other states. To improve my English, I picked up Christian magazines and looked at the pictures. Later, I began reading the news. Eventually, I began studying the schools and seminaries advertised in that magazine, and the desire to study in the United States germinated. Mrs. MacLean was good to me, and her children were kind. They would stop to talk to me while I worked, and sometimes the family gave me little gifts such as a toothbrush and toothpaste or pens and pencils at Christmas. They treated me well while I worked my way through school.

By 1974, I was nearly twenty years old and ready to move on to the next phase of my life, wherever the Lord would send me. But first, there was graduation, a time for students to celebrate with their families. As proud as I was of what I had accomplished, graduation was a day I wanted to avoid. Most of my classmates had bought new suits and new shoes and planned receptions. Many went out of their way to make the day extra special for themselves. I could do none of that. I had no money to shop for graduation or to plan for it as my friends were doing. I did not want to appear as the poorest in my class and therefore embarrass myself. I was ready to quietly miss the day and graduate *in absentia*. All I cared about was receiving my diploma and then getting out of there.

Mrs. MacLean stopped me one day when I was doing my chores. "Is your family coming to graduation?" she asked.

"No," I told her. "It's too far. There isn't enough money for them to make the trip."

Mrs. MacLean nodded. "But *you* are going to attend the ceremony." The way she said it, she made it sound as it were no longer optional that I attend.

Graduation was a formal event, attended by faculty, administrators, and students with their families as well as the mission leaders and even some local officials. All I had were the modest clothes I wore every day to school and work. If I attended graduation like that, I would embarrass myself.

"I don't have anything appropriate to wear," I said.

Mrs. MacLean smiled "Let's not worry about that."

Mrs. MacLean took me shopping and bought me a safari suit with trousers and a short-sleeved jacket made from a nice blue fabric. One of the teachers at the missionary school sold me a pair of second-hand shoes in my size: 14. They fit perfectly.

The day of my graduation, none of my classmates expected me—a poor Rwandan refugee who worked as a house servant—to be so well dressed. Although my family could not be there, the MacLeans attended my graduation and invited me to dine at their house that evening. That night I was a guest of their family.

My secondary education completed, I had achieved an important goal. But there was more for me to accomplish, especially if I wanted to pursue a life in ministry. College was the next step, but first I needed to find a job so I could earn tuition.

Doing well was not sufficient, as a refugee in a country that truly didn't want me there. I had to overcome the barriers of being a refugee. I had to excel. I had to do better than the rest. I was convinced that education would break the cycle of poverty for me, and that it would allow me to not only go as far as I could go but also help me rescue the rest of my family.

There were institutions of higher learning in Burundi, but my chances of being accepted were slim, given the quota system for Rwandan refugees. Even if I had been accepted, I needed tuition money, but I could not get a job in Burundi. I had no choice but to leave.

I left Mweya and made the trek back to the refugee settlement at Kigamba to see my family, where there was a small celebration for my high school graduation. I stayed three months, helping my parents and making my plans. My parents hoped I would stay and get a job, but they knew I had bigger ambitions. They knew there were limited opportunities for refugees in Burundi. They had to let me go.

Like the Israelites who were brought out of Egypt where they were enslaved, I had to trust that I, too, would one day be led to a promised land. I took heart in the stories from Exodus, how God heard and answered the prayers of his people, and His promise to lead them into a land flowing with milk and honey (Exodus, 3:16-17 NIV). At night, sitting around the fire, I plotted my future and considered where my own promised land would be. The East African countries, like Kenya, Tanzania, and Uganda, that had been under British colonial rule were better developed economically and had more colleges and universities than the French-speaking countries in central Africa, where I grew up. Since I spoke English, thanks to my time with the MacLean family and some classes at school, East Africa became my intended destination.

I had visited Tanzania while in secondary school at Mweya, and I could tell that the country was more advanced than Burundi. But Tanzania was in the midst of conversion to African socialism under the leadership of Julius Nyerere. Nyerere was very popular and admired by many, including me, but I was not sure how the country's socialism would impact career opportunities.

From what I read and heard about Kenya, there seemed to be more opportunities and therefore it became an attractive destination. The challenge was how to get there with no money, no connections, and no one to guide me. I had to trust that the Lord would provide the "pumpkins" along the way—food when I was hungry, money when my pockets were empty (which they were, most of the time), help when I needed it, and companions when I was lonely and in need of a friend.

I felt bad that I couldn't tell my mother where I was really going because I knew she would have tried to stop me. Who could blame her? I would be by myself, entering the unknown. I would be leaving my family behind, unsure if I would survive or perish, if I'd be killed by bad people or animals, or if I would die of hunger. And so I lied. One Friday in July 1974, I left, telling my family that I planned to visit my uncle who lived near the Burundi–Tanzania border, a day's journey from the Kigamba settlement. I was terrified, but I put on a brave face. So many thoughts—fear, possibilities, disbelief in myself, trust in God—mixed emotions that did not paralyze me, but, instead, challenged me to move on with my adventure. If I truly wanted a different life, I had no other alternative than to take the risk. The secret to combating my fears was my trust in God. Courage is not lack of fear, but rather "courage is fear that has said its prayers," as Karle Wilson Baker wrote in her poem "Courage."

As I left, my mother walked me part of the way, suspiciously asking me a million questions. I avoided making eye contact with her for fear that she would know I was lying and deduce the real purpose of my journey. Yes, I was going to visit my uncle, but while staying with him I was going to figure out a way, without money or travel documents, to get across the border and into Tanzania. And I would keep traveling after that, all the way to what I believed was my promised land for higher education: Kenya.

I walked out of the refugee settlement faster now, hoping my mother would stop escorting me, so I would not make her cry. If she had begun to weep at that moment, I would not have been able to contain my own tears. "Mom, you are delaying me," I said, coldly, and started running, knowing she could not keep up. I glanced behind me once at my mother standing in the path, watching me depart. Then I ran faster so that I could increase the distance between us and eliminate the pull to go back to the settlement with her. My heart was beating hard, tears were in my eyes, something twisted my throat hard as though I wanted to cry out loud, but I kept running, thinking that if I didn't die on my journey, someday I would come back and tell her the full story of my adventure and why I did it. I would be successful and provide for her; I would build her and my father a better house. Positive thinking pushed me into a different world, and, suddenly, my fear disappeared. I imagined a different life that I would live as result of my adventure and the success it would bring. My thoughts motivated me and kept me walking without feeling the fatigue of that day and the emotional drain that had captured me when I first left my mother behind.

I was off on a walking journey of 500 miles—with no money or means of travel, with only my faith to sustain me and a belief that the Lord would provide. I considered my trek an adventure with God. I drew my strength and courage from the Bible verses I had heard and memorized as a child. The words of the 23rd Psalm took on a deep and personal meaning: "The Lord is my shepherd, I lack nothing. He makes me lie down in green pastures, he leads me beside quiet waters, he refreshes my soul. He guides me along the right paths for his name's sake" (Psalm 23:1-3 NIV). I recited these verses to myself, over and over, especially when I began to feel apprehensive. "I lift up my eyes to the mountains—where does my help come from? My help comes from the Lord, the Maker of heaven and earth. He will not let your foot slip—he who watches over you will not slumber" (Psalm 121:1-3 NIV).

Growing up, these verses had held special meaning for me when I had to go into the bush to look for firewood or fetch water or when I had to venture deeper into the jungle in search of food. Now, as I was about to set out on a journey that would change my life forever, I had to believe that God was at my side. I could not venture beyond the confines of the refugee settlement if I did not know, deep in my soul, that God would provide for me, just as I remember He had when I was a child.

CHAPTER THREE

Exodus

"I lift up my eyes to the mountains—where does my help come from? My help comes from the Lord, the Maker of heaven and earth." (Psalm 121:1-2 NIV)

Traveling into the unknown was scary; being alone made it even more frightening, until I realized I was never alone. Each morning, I awoke with my Lord, and, at night, I went to sleep knowing God watched over me. Through my dependency on God, I experienced a deep relationship with Him. There was no one else on whom I could depend for food to eat, for water to drink, for shelter to sleep, for safety on unfamiliar roads. Each day was a walk in faith, believing that He would eventually bring me to my Promised Land: Kenya.

When I was alone, hungry, frightened, and unsure of how I would accomplish the next leg of the journey, sometimes my faith would be tested, but then I took stock of the many times the Lord had already provided for me, from the pumpkin that had saved me and my family during our starvation in the refugee camp to the many times that God sustained me on my journey with a friendly word from a stranger, a gift of food, companionship from fellow travelers, and a safe place to rest at night. Each time God met my needs yet again, often in the most unexpected ways, I made solemn promises in return: *If You get me where I need to go, if You open the doors I need to pass through, I will serve You. I will do whatever You want me to do in my life.*

Day by day, I had just enough to sustain me, which deepened my faith and trust as God showed me the depth of His love and boundless mercy. I recalled the words of Jesus in the Gospel of Luke as he urged his disciples not to worry "about your life, what you will eat; or about your body, what you will wear. For life is more than food, and the body more than clothes. Consider the ravens: They do not sow or reap, they have no storeroom or barn; yet God feeds them. And how much more valuable you are than birds! Who of you by worrying can add a single hour to your life? Since you cannot do this very little thing, why do you worry about the rest?" (Luke 12:22-26 NIV).

My journey had begun nearly two weeks previously when I left my family at the refugee settlement in Kigamba. From there, I walked a full day to the Mushiha refugee settlement near the Burundi–Tanzania border where I knew several Rwandan people, including one of my father's relatives who lived there. Although they were not expecting me, they opened their home to me and I spent a week there, learning all I could about how to cross the border into Tanzania

On market day, with so many people crossing the border to trade, it was easy for a traveler like me to blend in. So, I slipped into a crowd of people—men carrying baskets, women with bundles on their heads—and all of us walking from Burundi into Tanzania. It was so easy. I couldn't believe it! What had been built up in my mind as an impenetrable barrier had posed no obstacle. Certainly it would be the same at the Tanzanian and Kenyan borders.

The first town across the border in Tanzania was Nyaga-hura. Immediately, I went to the market to learn all I could about the travelers who came and went through this town. I heard about some Rwandans who lived in Tanzania and came to that market frequently to buy and resell used clothing—a very brisk trade in those days, some of it legal and some of it not. Tanzania restricted the flow of used clothing into the country to protect its fledgling garment industry. Soon, these traveling salespeople—I resist using the word smugglers—would become my companions and friends.

From Nyagahura I walked to Biharamuro, where I stayed with some Rwandans for a few days as I plotted the first leg of my journey to Kenya. Because Rwandan refugees tended to be very close knit, I was told about other Rwandans in the area. From place to place, I was told where to go, who to look up, and where I could probably stay. At each place, I also asked if there were Rwandan people there, as they would be my best bet for help. As refugees, we had an important commonality that gave us close kinship. People who have known the hardship of being outsiders are often very willing to give a helping hand to others. Surrounded by Rwandans who spoke my language, I felt welcomed by an extended family that opened its arms to embrace me. I thanked God for this sanctuary.

After several days, though, I was eager to press on to my next destination, the town of Geita on the shores of Lake Victoria, about 133 kilometers (83 miles) from Biharamuro. Water stretched beyond the horizon. Most wondrous and terrifying were the ferryboats that docked at Geita, carrying passengers, cars, small trucks, and even buses. I had never seen anything like these big flat boats with low sides, which made it appear as if the travelers were walking on water. The travelers were surrounded on all sides by water with no barriers to keep them from falling off. All I could think of was that I didn't know how to swim. To get to my next destination of Mwanza, I would have to ride such a ferry. It was a good thing I didn't have enough money to get on that ferry immediately, because I needed the extra time—more than a week—to work up the courage (and to earn enough money) to make the crossing.

By day, I walked around Geita looking for odd jobs to do. Being a lakeside town, Geita smelled like fish. But sometimes I got a whiff of something else: the mouth-watering aroma of food cooking. In the doorway of a small restaurant owned by some Tanzanian Somalis, I inhaled a tantalizing smell. I was so hungry, because of the meals I'd missed, because the sustenance I could get didn't hold me. I had eaten so little for so long, that every mouthful made the hole inside me feel even larger. I never had enough.

At this small restaurant, I stared at a man sitting alone at a table, just watching him eat, and hoping he would notice me and say, "Here, join me." I pulled myself away and walked around to gather myself. I returned to the restaurant and approached a man who looked like he might be the owner. "Excuse me," I asked politely. "Do you have a job I could do?"

The man sized me up, seeing that I was tall and strong. Perhaps he could also see something else in me; I was, like him, a stranger in that country. Rwandans and Somalis have a kinship and shared history of being refugees, which forged a bond as if we were countrymen. This Somali knew what it was to be vulnerable, which I surely was as I humbly stood in his restaurant doorway.

"Can you carry water?" he asked me.

"Of course," I replied.

I had seen many people carrying water in two buckets suspended from a long pole worn across their shoulders. It looked simple, but it was tricky to walk without it spilling all over. With the bar across my shoulders and a bucket suspended from each end, I had to keep my balance as I walked. Quickly, I got the hang of it and worked all day fetching water. I earned a little money and something to eat. It was heavenly to dip *amandazi,* a small doughnut, in a cup of tea, which melts in your mouth like a Krispy Kreme.

While I worked at the restaurant, I also kept my eye on the travelers who came to Geita, especially those who were getting on the ferry to Mwanza. If they could get on that thing and ride across the water, then so could I. After about a week at the restaurant, I had enough money for my fare and it was time to leave. Slowly I made my way onto the ferry with the other passengers, trying not to appear frightened. While the others stood along the side enjoying themselves, I sat on the deck, right in the middle of the ferry.

The engine revved and chugged as the ferry pulled away from the dock, but all I could hear was my pounding heart. The movement of the boat and the small waves on the lake made me dizzy, a sensation that soon turned to seasickness. There were so many people and vehicles onboard I couldn't imagine how that ferry could carry us all without sinking! I thought I was going to die before I ever set foot on firm ground again. After the longest hour of my life, Mwanza was in sight—a large city with high-rise buildings.

After I disembarked, I headed to the marketplace, which I knew from experience would be the safest place for a traveler alone and my best chance of meeting other Rwandans. As I walked through Mwanza, I listened carefully to strangers, hoping to hear a few words of my native language Kinyarwanda. When I heard only Swahili or other dialects, I kept quiet.

Mwanza had the biggest marketplace I had ever seen with so many things for sale, especially food: fruits and meats and flatbread. I spent two days and two nights in the market, figuring out my next move. My eyes were everywhere, watching the people as if it were a drama being staged just for me. On the third day, I came upon a group of about five people speaking mostly Swahili. Then I heard a few words of Kinyarwanda. I listened more closely; they were speaking my language! I approached them and, sure enough, they were Rwandans. Instantly, I felt a sense of home in this faraway place, and I knew I was being cared for by the Lord, who brings us peace that "transcends all understanding" (Phil. 4:7 NIV). Once again I was reminded that, by putting my trust in the Lord, I would find people to help me in my journey.

These Rwandans were also in the used clothing business, traveling frequently to Burundi to buy items to sell in Tanzania. Often they had to bribe bus drivers to hide their clothing bundles on top of the bus or in the carriers on the side. I came to see them as young men who, like me, were trying to make their way in the world. And, like me, they were refugees who never stopped thinking of themselves as Rwandan. Being displaced, facing hardships, being unwelcomed and sometimes ostracized in other countries made every Rwandan refugee like a brother or sister. In this spirit of kinship, they welcomed me and offered me a place to stay.

Soon Mwanza became a second home to me, a place I could have easily stayed, even joining my new friends in the second-hand clothing business. It was so very tempting, especially since these Rwandans seemed to be doing well for themselves. They had enough food to eat and could buy themselves things they needed; in comparison to me, they seemed prosperous. I always had a strong entrepreneurial streak and, given my previous experience back in Burundi selling pens, cigarettes, beer, and other small goods, I knew I could be a success in the clothing trade. I knew how to sell! Only one thing prevented me: my dream of getting an education so I could enter ministry. Surely God had not brought me that far just to have me enter the second-hand clothing trade! I had made a covenant with God, which made me strive beyond what was comfortable. To be of service to God, I had to leave my new friends and venture further into the unknown.

I spent a month in Mwanza, during which time I searched for answers to many of my questions: Who was going that way? Would they let me accompany them? What would happen when I had to cross the border into Kenya? Would it be as easy as going from Burundi to Tanzania? Or, would I face much tougher scrutiny since Kenya was a more developed country?

To fulfill my long-term plan, I had to focus first on these shorter-term concerns. Indeed, my journey to Kenya was comprised of many small steps. Even today, I follow the same pattern of making long-term plans while thriving on short-term wins. With each incremental gain, I am encouraged to keep going. As a leader, I strive to give others the same perspective. Every vision to be realized or goal to be accomplished can be broken down into smaller parts that must be tackled in sequence and then celebrated with each successive achievement. In this way, people learn from their accomplishments and gain knowledge that can be applied in the future, while also building strength and conviction that keeps them moving forward. Without embracing the short steps that make up a long journey, I would have given up somewhere in Tanzania and never reached my destination, and my vow to serve the Lord would have been left unfulfilled.

My next target was to get to the town of Musoma, about 225 kilometers (140 miles) away, located nearly equidistant between Mwanza and the Tanzania–Kenya border. Slowly, through my network of Rwandan refugee contacts, a plan emerged: A Rwandan who owned a restaurant in Musoma occasionally came to Mwanza; when he did, I would ask to accompany him to Musoma and work in his restaurant carrying water. All I had to do was be patient and wait.

One day, after several weeks, the man came to Mwanza and I was introduced to him. When I told him my story, he not only agreed to let me accompany him, he actually bought me a bus ticket. This offer was so unexpected, so generous, its equivalent today would be someone giving me a ride in a private jet. The bus was big, with comfortable seats and music playing. This was traveling first class! As we rolled through towns along the way, people ran up to the bus to sell us bananas, peanuts, and other small things through the windows. My generous traveling companion made sure we both had what we needed.

I stayed in Musoma for a month and a half, working for this man, whose name, unfortunately, I can no longer remember, but whose offer to help I've never forgotten. I earned a little money and planned for the next phase of my journey to the town of Tarime. Getting there, though, meant crossing the Serengeti, which means "endless plains." As I would learn much later, the Serengeti draws visitors from around the world to see the wildlife migration. To me, the thought of crossing those dry "endless plains" where lions hunted brought only fear and one obvious conviction: I was not going to walk.

When I told my plan to my Rwandan friend who had taken me to Musoma, he once again gave me a generous gift: He bought my bus ticket to Tarime.

On that bus ride, I saw every kind of animal imaginable: wildebeests, zebras, elephants, lions, buffaloes, gazelles, and more. I was on a safari before I knew the meaning of the word. Years later, I would hear my American friends talk about their dreams of going on safari one day or else they would share photos from their adventures on the Serengeti plains. For them, it was a fantasy come true. For me, in those days, I was trying to get to school in Kenya and the Serengeti was just something in my way that had to be crossed.

The Serengeti, though, wasn't the only wild place. Tarime, too, had a wild side that caught me, an unworldly young man, completely unaware. It was nighttime when the bus pulled into Tarime. Sleeping in the outdoor market would not be an option, as Tarime was not a big town, and there weren't the swarms of travelers as I had seen elsewhere. Fortunately, I had a little money to pay for a modest room at a travelers' lodge. I had changed money at the border in order to enter Kenya, and a woman took my Kenyan shillings and showed me to a small room. As I lay on a narrow bed, trying to get some sleep, I was kept awake by persistent knocking on my door. My mind raced with possibilities: I had been followed from the bus station to this place where someone intended to rob me of what little I had. I might even be killed just for being a refugee, a displaced person in a country that did not want him. I was alone in the wilderness, in a terrible little lodge near the bus station. To keep myself safe, I pushed the few pieces of furniture in the room against the door and waited for sunrise. Finally, morning came.

The lodge I had stayed at was actually a brothel. Prostitutes had knocked on my door all night long, thinking I was a customer. Once we understood each other—I just wanted a room and to be left alone—I could stay at that lodge in peace. But it wouldn't be for very long. From Tarime, I could literally see my Promised Land. Kenya lay just beyond the border.

On the Tanzania side was a dirt road; on the Kenyan side, the road was paved. Immigration officers from each country manned stations on either side of the border. Crossing here, I told myself, wasn't going to be as easy as walking from Burundi to Tanzania.

I spent four days in Tarime observing the border crossing, seeing how people made their way from one country to another. Without travel documents to show the Tanzanian officials on one side and Kenyan immigration on the other, I didn't see how I would make it. I could not give up after coming this far and refused to let my fear defeat me. Surely the Lord who parted the Red Sea for the Israelites would find a way for one Rwandan refugee to make his way into Kenya. As St. Paul wrote in his letter to the Romans, "If God is for us, who can be against us?" (Romans 8:31 NIV). I held tightly to the belief that God was for me.

Finally, I gathered up the courage to confide in a man I had become acquainted with. "I want to cross into Kenya."

"Where did you come from?" he asked me.

I told him that I had come from Mwanza. My destination was the nearest town over the border in Kenya.

"You mean Migori," the man said.

"Yes. How do I get there?"

"You just show your Tanzanian identification on this side and do the same on the other side, in Kenya," he explained.

I swallowed hard. I didn't have any Tanzanian identification. The only document I had was my old high school ID card from Burundi, which would hardly suffice to travel from one country to another. Then I remembered the strategy that had served me well before.

"When is market day in Migori?" I asked.

"Saturday," he said.

I smiled and nodded. That would be the day of my deliverance into Kenya.

That paved road on Kenya's side and the smart uniforms worn by the Kenyan immigration officers spoke to me of greater efficiency and a desire to keep out vagrants with no business crossing the border into their country. Immigration officers were stationed on both sides of the border. Even if I managed to get out of Tanzania without question, surely the Kenyan officials would stop me. But, papers or no papers, I had to try. Saturday came and, sure enough, a stream of people began to flow along the dirt road on the Tanzanian side of the border, loaded with baskets and bundles bound for the market. As I watched, the first few who traveled in small groups were stopped to show their papers. But as the crowds thickened, I noticed, those who were obviously bound for the market—a day trip that would take them over the border and back—were waved across. All I had to do was make it appear that I was part of that throng of people going to the market.

I gathered up my small satchel and slung it on my shoulder, as if it might be full of goods to sell. Then I fell in step with a crowd of people walking toward the border. To my amazement, no one stopped us. The border guards just waved us all past. I didn't look left or right; I didn't walk fast or slow. I just kept moving with the pace of the others as if we belonged together, watching the road under my feet turn from the dirt of Tanzania to the pavement of Kenya. I took my first steps in the Promised Land.

Small buses called *matutu* passed me, but I was out of money again, so there was no option except to walk the three hours to Migori. As I traveled along the shoulder, a bus rumbled by me. On the front was a sign for destination: Nairobi. A chill of recognition rippled through me. I really was in Kenya.

Along the way, I encountered an older gentleman. As we talked, I told him I was trying to get to Migori, but didn't have enough money for the *matutu*. Taking pity on me, a poor traveler, he gave me the ten shillings and I flagged down the next bus. I was in Migori in no time and headed immediately to the town square, which was open and wide like a soccer field, with shops around the perimeter. I assessed it to be a safe place where I could stay overnight, but my prayer was to find a Rwandan or a Somali who would give me a job in a restaurant, chopping wood or fetching water. My primary objective, though, was finding something to eat.

As I walked around, I spied a restaurant with a Somali name. Relying on the kinship between Rwandans and Somalis, I told the owners I was Rwandan and had come from Mwanza—all the while trying to prove that I was not a desperate or dangerous person.

"Sit down," the owner told me, gesturing toward one of the small tables in the restaurant. He turned to a waiter and spoke in Swahili: "Bring him tea."

"There is someone you should meet," the owner told me. "He is Rwandan and a teacher."

And so I waited for this man, sipping my tea. My eyes were everywhere, especially at the food being brought out of the kitchen and put in front of the other customers. I was so hungry I thought I would not last the day. "O Lord," I prayed silently. "You have provided for me on the journey. I need something to eat. Please let them bring something . . ." Politeness kept me from asking the owner for something; I was a stranger, but not a beggar. And so I prayed for the patience and forbearance to wait for this Rwandan man without really knowing why. After two hours, a light-skinned man walked into the restaurant. He didn't look Rwandan: his hair and beard were softer and curly, more in line with the Somali style.

"Vitalis!" the restaurant owner announced. "Here is a countryman of yours! He's been waiting for you."

I stood to greet him in the traditional Rwandan fashion of a handshake and a hug. As I introduced myself, I gave him a little of my recent travel history, back to Musoma in Tanzania. Vitalis knew that town well and even the restaurant where I worked for a month. His parents, he told me, were living in Tanzania near the border of Burundi, an area I knew well. After he mentioned a man named Joseph and his brother, Charles, who had been among my Rwandan friends in Mwanza, we were soon trading names and stories about mutual friends and acquaintances.

"Come, let's have some tea," Vitalis said excitedly. He turned to the waiter to order.

I accepted another cup of tea and hoped deep down that the waiter would bring more than one pastry. Sure enough, the waiter brought four pastries—two for each of us—and I offered a silent prayer of thanks to the Lord not only for the food but also for this new friend.

As we shared tea and pastries, Vitalis told me a little about his life in Migori. He was a schoolteacher and his wife was Rwandan, from Burundi. I explained that I had been traveling for five months already, en route to Nairobi to fulfill my dream of attending Bible college. Knowing I had no place to say, he invited me to spend the night with him and his wife.

Vitalis paid for our tea and pastries, and we walked together out of the restaurant. We took a *matatu* to his village, and, after getting off the bus, we went about 500 yards when we saw a woman with a baby in her arms. Vitalis waved to her in greeting and we kept walking. When we got close enough that I could see his wife's face, I knew she was familiar. Suddenly, she started running toward me and we embraced. Vitalis looked more surprised than shocked, and we quickly explained that we had known each other as children, back at the Kigama refugee settlement in Burundi. The little row house her parents lived in had been just two over from ours. Her name was Epephanie, and she was a couple of years older than me. I had been a sophomore in high school the last time I saw her. Now she was standing in Kenya with her husband and child.

Together, the three of us headed to their home where Epephanie boiled water so I could bathe. That night we ate potatoes and cassava and talked until one in the morning. By the time we went to bed, they had heard all about my journey, from the time I left Burundi through my travels in Tanzania and now, finally, in Kenya.

"Don't worry," Vitalis told me that night. "You are safe here. You can make this your place for as long as you wish."

I fell asleep praising God that He had, once again, provided for me in profound and mysterious ways.

Over the next month with Vitalis, Epephanie, and their child, I became part of a family. I could not find a job there, so each morning I accompanied Vitalis when he went to school, then walked around the town. Toward the end of the school day, I would go to the teashop and wait for him there, and we went home together. On the weekends, we all spent time together. I got stronger and healthier and put on some weight.

Vitalis and I discussed the last leg of my journey to Nairobi—how I would get there and what I would do to attend Bible college.

"I need to get a job in the city so I can go to university," I told him.

"First, you need to register with the U.N. High Commissioner for Refugees," Vitalis explained. "You need to document your status as a Rwandan refugee in Kenya."

That sounded daunting to me, especially since I had no travel documents or other identification. Vitalis assured me that all would work out: "There are other Rwandans in Nairobi. We'll find a way for you to contact them."

In those cozy times at their modest house, those plans were only in the talking stage. It was becoming harder to think of pulling up stakes and moving on from people who had become as close to me as my own siblings. But as 1974 came to a close, Vitalis and his wife received word from his family that they had to go back to Tanzania for a while. Their departure, I knew, also marked my send-off. Too soon, we hugged as they went off to Tanzania and I formulated my departure plan for Nairobi.

With no money for bus fare, I asked the Somali restaurateur for a job, but he didn't hire me. When Vitalis found out, he gave me forty shillings for travel expenses. The money was more than enough for bus fare to Nairobi, but I decided to stretch it by traveling instead in a small pickup truck that carried passengers for a modest fee. Only when we were on the road did I discovered that we weren't going to Nairobi, but in another direction. I got off at the next town, changed to a *matutu,* and finally ended up in Ahero—the wrong place, with no idea of how to get to Nairobi. I had spent all of those forty shillings and, once again, I was out of money. In my foolishness and confusion, I felt lost and forlorn, made all the worst by the gnawing hunger in my stomach that made it difficult to think straight.

The aroma of roasted corn wafted across the town. Although smelling it was torture, I had to follow my nose, even though I had no way of buying any. I found an old woman tending a fire in the market with several ears of corn on a grate. She looked at me, and our eyes locked. Without a word, she gave me an ear of corn. I grabbed it with both hands and started eating, without even saying thank you.

"Where are you going?" she asked.

"Nairobi," I replied between gulps.

That woman—neither Rwandan nor Somali, who had no obvious kinship to me—reached in her pocket and gave me seventeen shillings for bus fare. As if in a dream, I took the money and headed to the bus station, where I bought a ticket for Nairobi.

What had she seen in me that moved her to give me an ear of corn, which was how she supported herself and her family, plus the money for the bus? Was she moved by my hunger and poverty? Did she have a son my age? Or was she like the Good Samaritan who took pity on the traveler who had been robbed and beaten, paying for his lodging and care?

Reflecting on this chance encounter, I recognize that this woman was yet another "pumpkin" provided mysteriously and miraculously by God. If there is no other message to take from this testimony of mine, it is this: Trust in the Lord and you will never be forsaken. At times it will be difficult. You may feel abandoned and even suffer. But God will provide for you. Even if you have to wait on the Lord, take heart: God's timing is perfect, and He is never late.

CHAPTER FOUR

The Promised Land

"And I have promised to bring you up out of your misery in Egypt into . . . a land flowing with milk and honey." (Exodus 3:17 NIV)

Early 1975

Begging is an interesting endeavor. With no other choice for survival, on my first day in Nairobi—my Promised Land—it was the only thing I could do. Nairobi was a large and dangerous city. Even the 24/7 bustling bus station was intimidating. Massive buildings, none the size I had ever seen before, seemed to whirl around me as I became dizzy from hunger. It had been a day and a half since my last bite of food. The city was so intimidating that I didn't know where to start looking for a job. My first priority was to get something to eat. I had to swallow my pride and learn how to beg.

To beg, I had to size people up. Did he look generous? Did she seem kind? If I asked for something, would they give it to me or send me off like a stray dog? Though dirty and tattered from traveling, I politely asked those that fit my makeshift profile: "I am hungry. Do you have five shillings to spare so I can buy something to eat?"

Most people would give me a few cents. When I had enough, I bought a banana or corn on the cob grilled with mild pepper spices, which tasted so good. (To this day, when I go to Nairobi, I make sure to get a grilled corn on the cob from a street vendor.) Sometimes the vendor would take pity on me and give me extra, especially if I was buying bananas. I'd eat one immediately, but always saved the other for later, because I never could be sure when I would eat again.

Unlike the smaller towns where I could stay in the marketplace, there were no such safe havens for me in Nairobi. Instead, I lived in the bus station. Because there were so many buses there, I had no problem finding an empty one to sit in and sleep for a short while. Paying passengers often boarded the buses early to make sure they got a seat before it became too crowded, even if that meant napping on them. I would board the bus, too, as if I were going somewhere. Some of the bus drivers didn't mind because they liked their buses to appear fuller, which would make people buy a ticket sooner. But when the conductor started hitting the side of the bus, the signal to passengers that it was time to depart, I had to rush off and move to a different one. I rotated from bus to bus, trying to catch a little sleep before going out again to beg for something to eat.

I had been begging at the bus station for two weeks. The longer I stayed in the bus station, the more discouraged I became. Filled with negative thoughts and regret, soon my mind began to fear I would die there. I had to find work to support myself. Until I had money for food and shelter, I could not pursue my objective of furthering my education at Bible college. I ventured deeper into the city to see where I might ask for a job.

Ahead I saw a sign: Hotel Ambassadeur. Given its French

name, I thought that, because I spoke French fluently, perhaps I could get hired there. But as I got closer, I realized it was a fancy hotel with a restaurant on an outside veranda and nice tables covered with white cloths. From where I stood across the street, I could see employees in uniforms and well-dressed guests. One look at my dirty rags and they'd throw me into the street for sure. And yet I could think of no other plan. As tired, hungry, and discouraged as I was, I refused to give in to the fear that God had led me all that way just to abandon me in Nairobi. Quitting had not been an option before, so why should it be now? Call it risk-taking, determination, the relentless pursuit of my goals, or walking by faith—and, truthfully, it was a combination of all of them. Always I was goaded to keep on, never to give up, even when I was tempted to do so.

I stood on the corner opposite that hotel for hours, trying to summon my courage. As I waited, two men deeply engrossed in conversation approached the corner and waited to cross the street. I overheard some of their words. "You're speaking Kinyarwanda," I said excitedly. They also looked Rwandan.

Shocked, they turned to me as if I were from another planet. Pointing at me, one man warned the other, "He is Kikuyu," referring to a large ethnic group of people in Kenya who were farmers and herdsmen. In an accusatory tone, the man continued, glaring at me with disdain, "He has learned our language and is trying to get money from us." Quickly, they moved away from me.

"No!" I protested, "I am Rwandan." I began to follow the men, desperate to convince them that I was a countryman and meant them no harm. One of them swore and told me to leave them alone.

As they walked away, I heard one man call the other a familiar name. "I know you!" I yelled and then gave the names of his father, brother, and sister, as well as my own father's name. They stopped and stared at me, recognition growing between us. Like me, they had been refugees in Burundi. "Your father, he was the teacher," one of them said to me.

Tears of joy and deliverance filled my eyes. They knew my father and they knew me. Never would I forget that moment of grace when I, an outcast, became embraced. Filthy, hungry, and completely alone, I had almost despaired, but once again the Lord delivered me. As I accompanied my two countrymen to their home, I told them how I made the trip all the way from Burundi. They knew my friend, Vitalis, who lived at the border, and our connection grew even stronger.

These Rwandans were poor, but shared what they had with me. In all my travels around the world, I have observed that Rwandans tend to welcome their own—an expression of Rwandan spirit, kinship, and solidarity, especially among the refugee victims of the massacres carried out by pre-1994 governments.

The men told me they received a small stipend from the UNHCR, which helped pay for their schooling: One was studying electrical work and the other, sewing. Remembering what Vitalis had told me, I knew I needed to register with the Commissioner as well.

I lived with my compatriots for three months. After their school, we would walk to downtown Nairobi, where they liked to drink and socialize. I didn't drink a drop, but I was happy to be with them. One day, I decided to go on my own to Uhuru Park, a large recreational park near the central business district. On this particular day, it was late afternoon, and in the park were people listening to music and preaching the gospel. It had been almost six months since I had heard people preaching on the street to a group.

When the man preaching concluded the sermon, I approached him and shared my plan to become a minister. Clearly the Lord had led me to the right person because he told me he worked for the Bible Society of Kenya. From his briefcase, he pulled out a list of all the Christian colleges in Kenya and the missions they belonged to. My eyes immediately focused on Kenya Highlands Bible College, which was supported by the World Gospel Mission. I knew this organization because, back in Burundi, it had brought my father to the Lord.

Kenya Highlands Bible College was located in Kericho, which was known for its tea plantations, about 250 kilometers (180 miles) away.

That night I excitedly shared my plans with my friends. They were happy for me, but no one had any money to get me there. So I traveled by the only means I had: on foot. I walked by day and, at night, stayed in bus stands. The road between Nairobi and Kericho was dangerous. Many times I saw zebras, lions, and hyenas roaming nearby, but I did not fear because I felt the Lord near me at all times. When I needed courage, I recalled the scriptures and counted on the Lord. My favorite was always the 23rd Psalm: "Even though I walk through the valley of the shadow of death, I will fear no evil for you are with me; your rod and your staff, they comfort me" (Psalm 23:4 NIV).

When I finally arrived at Kericho Township, I went to the College principal's house, knocked, and waited at the doorway to my future. Once inside, my life's dream would become a reality. I was reminded of the promise in the Gospel of

Matthew: "Ask and it will be given to you; seek and you will find; knock and the door will be opened to you" (Matthew 7:7 NIV).

An American woman came to the entrance, but kept the screen door closed between us. We spoke together in English.

"My name is Laurent Mbanda, and I have come here from Burundi," I began. "I am Rwandan."

"From what tribe?" she asked.

"Tutsi," I replied.

She turned around and left me outside for a good twenty minutes. Finally she returned. "I cannot help you. We need to take you into town and find you a place to stay."

I was stunned. I hadn't even been allowed to cross the threshold and tell her one thing about myself other than my nationality and ethnicity.

The woman put a coat on and went outside. Two watchmen approached me, one carrying a big stick and the other a machete. The woman drove a van up to the door. The two watchmen opened the back and told me to get in.

Fear gripped me. I could not imagine what I had done to be treated this way. The woman was so tense, and the two watchmen looked ready to strike me at any moment. There had to be some mistake. The van stopped in front of the police station.

"I am an innocent man," I pleaded. "I know many missionaries from the World Gospel Mission." I recited every name I could think of. The woman, however, remained unmoved.

The Kenyan police asked me for my passport. I shook my head. They asked for travel documents; I didn't have any. I handed over my old student identification card from Burundi.

"How did you cross from Burundi to Tanzania and then into Kenya without papers?" they demanded.

I shrugged and hung my head. My story would not interest them.

They locked me in a jail cell—a filthy place smelling of urine, with dirty, cold cement floors, broken windows with iron bars, and no furniture of any kind. Groups of prisoners spoke among themselves in Swahili; from what I could make out, they complained about their arrests and screamed out to guards as they passed, begging for cigarettes. I was terrified.

Alone, a stranger in a foreign country without any papers or anyone to speak for me, I knew that I could very easily "disappear" from that jail and never be heard from again. Hour after hour, I was sure I would be killed by the guards or the other prisoners, some of whom looked so strange to me. They had pierced ears and large earrings and ear ornaments and no lower front teeth. Later, I learned they were Kipsigis, nomadic people who were part of the larger Kalenjin tribe.

In the dark night, I tried to pray, but the words were like sand in my mouth. My fears amplified in my mind: *I am finished. They will kill me in the morning.* Even if I had a place to sleep, there was no way I could. The coldness of the highlands crept into my bones, and I shivered the entire night.

Early the next day, as I waited in my cell, I saw a white woman at the jail, speaking to the guards in their local language; she seemed to be highly respected by them. But I was so exhausted and distraught from my long ordeal overnight, I did not recognize her. The police brought her to my cell.

"I know who he is," she told them.

To me, she added, "You are innocent."

The woman was Dr. Eva Gilger, who was the administrator of the Kenya Highlands Bible College. The night before, during a missionary radio call, Dr. Gilger spoke with an American from World Gospel Mission who was stationed in

Burundi and told him my name. He remembered me; I had been one of his students.

She explained that she had mistaken me for someone else who was a threat to one of the teachers. After a long night, during which I prepared myself spiritually and emotionally for the very real possibility of being killed, I stepped into the morning light of freedom.

Dr. Gilger brought me back to the school and spoke the words I had waited so long to hear: "We will admit you. But there is a catch. We need you to produce your former school transcript." She explained the application process and told me everything I needed to do. Then she drove me back to town and booked a room for me. She gave me 150 Kenyan shillings for bus fare to Burundi. "Get the papers you need and come back," she said. This trip would be far easier than the six-month trek that had gotten me there.

The next morning, full of resolve and optimism, I bought a ticket and got on a bus that reversed the route I took to get to Kenya. From Kenya we drove to Tanzania; when I crossed the border, I changed my money into Tanzanian shillings. Then we went all the way to Mwanza. I took another bus to the Burundi border of Kobero in Muyinga Province, where I exchanged my Tanzanian shillings for Burundi francs. From the border, I had to walk 25 kilometers (about 15.5 miles) before I could find public transportation to the capital city of Bujumbura, in hopes of getting a passport. Unfortunately, I did not know the process for refugees like me, who needed to apply for what were called "travel documents," which were issued in cooperation with the U.N. High Commissioner for Refugees.

It took three months to get my documentation, during which time I stayed with some distant relatives who could afford to feed me only one meal a day—and sometimes not even that. Yet I am grateful to them for taking me in; without them, those long and difficult months in Bujumbura would have been excruciating. I am also so grateful to a worker named George who was kind to me and tried to help, by suggesting what I needed to do to navigate the process more easily to obtain my travel documents. At the time, he did not reveal himself to be a fellow Rwandan, most likely to protect his job. But for me, he was in the right place at the right time.

Because I had used up the little money left over from my inbound trip, I had to go around to my extended family members to raise enough money for a ticket back to Kenya. Then I visited my old high school to request a sealed transcript be sent directly to Kenya Highlands Bible College. While I was there, I learned that the headmaster at the school had recently visited Kenya Highlands and that when Dr. Gilger mentioned my name to him, he had tried to discourage them from admitting me. While I can only guess the headmaster's motives, I surmise that he wanted to keep me in Burundi. The assumption was always that if someone went out of the country, he or she would not return to serve their own country. Also, during this era of colonial missionaries, most local missionaries were not supportive of higher education. Therefore, he may very well have thought that if I became highly educated, I would not return to serve the church.

Convinced that the high school was not going to send my transcript, I went to my former teachers and asked them for help. They couldn't get an official transcript for me, but one of the teachers was able to obtain a copy of my last report card, which he put into an envelope with a seal from the school.

When I returned to Kericho, Dr. Gilger seemed surprised to see me.

"Here, I have my travel documents." I put the papers on her desk. "And here is the report card from my last year in school to prove that I graduated with good grades."

Dr. Gilger sat back in her chair. Clearly, she had not expected me to return. Little did she know that getting a few papers and raising money for a bus ticket was nothing compared to my ordeal of first getting to Kenya! Now that I was standing in her office, Dr. Gilger couldn't turn me away.

"We will admit you," she told me finally. "But on probation." When I asked Dr. Gilger to explain, she told me tuition was $450 a year. "I want to know how you are going to get that money."

I responded with what I believed, because of everything I had been through: "God will provide."

Dr. Gilger put up her hand. "Students say this to me all the time. But I am not God. You have to find the money."

It was July 1975, and I was admitted to Kenya Highlands Bible College. No matter that I was on probation—I was finally in school! The administration gave me two months to pay my tuition, but I had no idea where I would get the money. My English was also very poor. When I sat in classes, I did not understand much of what was said, so I got notes from other students and studied very hard. I did very well in my homework, even though I was the worst English speaker.

Since Kenya had been a British colony, at school we followed the English tradition of tea at four o'clock. But one day, before teatime, Dr. Gilger called me aside. "The two months are up. You have to pay the tuition. Do you have the money?"

I shook my head. "I don't have any money."

"Then you have to leave school." Dr. Gilger didn't even allow me to have four o'clock tea.

I left Dr. Gilger's office, walked to the men's dormitory, went into my room, and lay down on my bed. I cried and prayed until, emotionally and physically exhausted, I fell asleep. When I awoke, I wandered outside. I sat on the ground, leaning up against a tree. A fellow student named Solomon was walking the grounds, meditating and praying. When he saw me and noticed how distressed I was, Solomon offered to pray with me.

"I don't need your prayers," I told him. "I have already prayed and prayed, but God is not listening." I got up and walked away. Returning to the dormitory, I went to my room and stayed there the rest of the day. The next morning, Dr. Gilger came to the entrance of the men's dormitory. Unable to enter that building, she stood outside and called my name.

"Praise the Lord! Praise the Lord!" Dr. Gilger exclaimed when she saw me.

I had no idea what she was talking about.

"You have a gift from America," she told me.

I was more confused than ever. "Someone has given $300 for you to go to school, and I will make sure that the remaining $150 is provided for you."

The explanation she gave astounded me. On the missionary radio call the night before, Dr. Gilger had shared my plight with the other missionaries who had served or were serving in Africa, among them a man named Harold Shingledecker, who at the time was on furlough in Marian, Indiana. After hearing my story, he shared the details with members of his church. This story reached Nancy Proctor Grimes in Lafayette, Indiana, who had been to Burundi as a missionary and knew Mrs. MacLean, who had hosted me when I was a high school student in Burundi. Nancy pledged $300 to help keep me in school. Within two weeks, the Lord provided the other $150 through other donations.

With my first full-year tuition paid, I resumed my studies with enthusiasm. Dr. Gilger and I also came up with a plan for me to earn extra money by chopping wood, washing missionaries' cars, and cutting grass around campus. For the second year's tuition, I prayed for God to show me how to find funding. Later, I learned that the All-Africa Conference of Churches (AACC), which was headquartered in Nairobi, had a department for refugees. I wrote a letter requesting a scholarship and was promised enough money to pay all three years of my remaining tuition. Once again, the Lord provided for me.

By the time I was finishing my senior year of Bible college in 1979 in Kenya, Burundi had begun expelling foreign missionaries. Missionaries were accused of inciting a rebellion against the military-led government at that time. Some of these people came through Kenya on their way home, and a few of them who knew me sought me out at Kenya Highlands. They told me of the great need for local teachers at missionary schools. Given that I had grown up as a refugee in Burundi surely there would be a place for me, now that I had received my education. One of the places that was in desperate need of teachers was Mweya Bible School, located outside of Gitega in central Burundi, where I had received my secondary education.

In order to take advantage of this opportunity, I had to leave school early while I still had one course to complete. The school administration made arrangements for an independent study for me, which enabled me to graduate a term early with a bachelor's degree.

There was one final wrinkle in my plans to graduate: When it came time for me to leave, Kenya Highlands did not want to give me my diploma because my tuition was unpaid. Although I had received a scholarship from AACC, the College did not want to accept money from that organization because it was not "evangelical enough." The refusal by the College to accept money from the AACC, however, did not change the fact that I had obtained tuition money from a reputable source. It was not my fault that the College would not accept it. In the end, I was given my diploma—even though three years of tuition went unpaid.

As I prepared to return to Burundi, I was excited about the prospect of becoming a teacher in a missionary school. Here was the perfect opportunity to serve the Lord, while also preparing myself for future education. All along, my secret desire was to one day go to the United States or somewhere in Europe to pursue an advanced degree. I held fast to this dream because I saw education as not only preparation for my near-term future, but also the key to breaking the cycle of poverty and securing a better future. All I had to do was get back to Burundi and apply for a job that had been all but promised to me by those missionaries who were leaving.

A windfall soon came my way. When I told the AACC about the College's refusal to accept their scholarship money, the AACC told me that they would give the money to me instead. What a gift! I was able to buy clothing, shoes, and a ticket on an Air France flight from Nairobi to Burundi—my first time flying, which was quite an experience.

Convinced that the Mweya school opportunity was an answer to a prayer, I arrived at Bujumbura where I spent a day and a half with family and friends who welcomed me home. My parents and siblings were still living in the refugee settlement upcountry. All along that 15-kilometer (about 9 miles) route to the school, I talked excitedly about Kenya, my studies, and eagerness to begin teaching at Mweya. The clergyman who drove me listened, but did not say much. I was too excited to notice.

The moment I arrived, I sensed something was off. No one welcomed me. Instead, they started to grill me with questions. "How did you learn of this teaching opportunity? Who told you what was happening here?"

I explained that I had met some of the expatriate missionaries in Kenya before they traveled back to the States. "Since I now have my degree, they told me I should come back here to teach," I said, convinced that this straightforward and honest answer would satisfy them. Instead, they remained guarded.

"We have no money to pay you," they told me. "Do you have supporters who will provide your salary?"

Immediately, I assured them that, if money were an issue, I would work for no salary. "I am willing to take up the challenge with faith that the Lord will provide," I told them.

From the looks on their faces, I could tell that this was not the response they had expected. To tell the truth, I was surprised by my own words. "Oh, we can't do that," they told me. "It would not be right to have you work here without being able to pay you."

Again, I assured them that I would not let a lack of salary stand in my way.

Then their questioning turned more pointed and political. "We heard that you said things in Kenya that were negative toward the people of Burundi and especially the Hutus."

I denied it. "Who would I have said such a thing to?" I asked them. Many of my fellow students in Kenya were from that ethnic group, as were many government and church leaders. "If I held that view, which I do not, I would never have come back here to teach," I said.

Every time I answered the school administrators' questions, someone wrote down my responses, which made me nervous. Who knew if they were recording them accurately or only writing down what suited their purposes?

When they asked me another question, I ended the interview. There was no reason for me to continue to be grilled about fabricated rumors. I thanked them for the opportunity to meet with them and got up to leave. I hoped that the man from my home church who had driven me to the school would give me a ride back to town.

"You can walk," he told me.

His response not only crushed me, it also sent a shock wave of fear through me. Was I going to be the target of some violence on the road? I left immediately and started walking the 15 kilometers back to town. On the way, I met an American missionary woman who asked me about the outcome of the meeting. I could read the disappointment in her face when I told her they had no intention of hiring me because of political reasons. Here was further proof of how much the Rwandan refugees were hated by some of the Burundi people and the government at the time.

With every step I took on the way back to town, my regrets intensified. I had been so enthusiastically encouraged to come to Burundi to take this job that I had left Kenya in a hurry, spending almost all my money on an airplane ticket and new clothing for my teaching position. I had very little left to sustain myself. Those 15 kilometers back to town felt longer to me than the entire six months of trekking from Burundi to Kenya. When I got to Gitega, I immediately got public transportation to Bujumbura, where I stayed with relatives and looked for a job.

Once again, I was confronted by prejudice. Every job was for Burundians first. Foreigners—even refugees who had lived almost all their lives in Burundi—had to get clearance from the Ministry of Labor, which was difficult to obtain. Frustrated and regretful, I went to visit my parents and family members in the refugee settlement near the Tanzanian border. It was so hard to go there empty-handed, instead of with gifts for everyone as part of a great celebration. One day, I told myself, I would do it. I stayed with them for a week and then returned to Bujumbura.

As I weighed my options, I considered all the skills I had acquired by God's grace in Kenya. Since I spoke French and English, I thought I might be able to support myself by teaching English as a second language. I approached a British missionary named Roger Bowen with the Anglican Church of Burundi with the idea of offering English classes at the church's community center. He liked the idea, and we teamed up to start afternoon and evening classes. In addition, I took on some private students, including a couple of people from the Burundi Army who planned to go to the States and a husband and wife, Mr. and Mrs. Gaetan Nikobamye, who ran a business selling automobiles. They were very loving and caring toward me, even though we came from different tribal backgrounds. Tribal lines, I believe, can be transcended.

Little by little, I earned enough to support myself and rent a modest apartment. Yet, I continued to be preoccupied by thoughts about my future. Should I go back to Kenya for graduate school? Should I look into other universities? As I investigated the possibilities, I developed relationships with missionaries, expatriates from a variety of countries, and other missions. (Today, they call this networking, which I love to do and consider it one of my strongest skills.)

Then one day, around the end of November 1979, I received a letter from a college friend with the most unexpected news. He had recommended me for a job with Campus Crusade, an interdenominational evangelical organization that ministers to university students and to churches in some parts of the world. Campus Crusade (now called Cru) was hosting a conference in Kinshasa, the capital of what was then known as Zaire (today the Democratic Republic of the Congo), and needed people who were bilingual in French and English to work as translators.

I waited with excitement to hear from Campus Crusade. I didn't know much about the organization at the time, but here was a chance at last to work in ministry and to leave Burundi. Just as my friend had promised, I was invited to the conference. Before I could go to Kinshasa for the conference, however, I needed the recommendation from my church leader—the same man who had turned me down for the job at Mweya school in Gitega. Surely if the regional leadership of Campus Crusade was asking him to do this for me, he would comply. I went to Gitega to see him about a recommendation, but he told me he wasn't ready. "Come back another time," he said.

I knew what this meant. He either wanted a bribe or was using evasive tactics to refuse the recommendation. In the practical reality of how it was in Burundi then, saying "come back another time" meant the person was letting you think for yourself how to get him to do what you wanted done. I was not about to bribe him, regardless of how much I needed the recommendation. However, I was willing to "come back" at least prove a point—and I did. The answer was still the same: "Come back another time." I knew for sure he wanted me to come back with something.

I waited until he was coming to Bujumbura and saw him at a guest house that belonged to the church. "Can you help me?" I asked.

"I don't have the means to write that letter," he told me.

"You can write it by hand," I assured him.

"I don't have paper and a pen," he replied, even though I could see a pen in his pocket.

"I will get some paper and a pen if you are willing to write it," I insisted.

He shook his head. "No, that's not how things are done."

Every effort I made to get a recommendation from another church leader resulted in one rejection after another. In my mind I could not help but feel victimized and hated simply because of who I was—a refugee, a man who was stateless for reasons not of my making. It made me wonder whether these ministers had a true calling to serve others. I could not believe another opportunity within my grasp was about to be taken away—except I was determined, and I had faith that the Lord, once again, would provide.

CHAPTER FIVE

Plan B

"Blessed are you when people insult you, persecute you and falsely say all kinds of evil against you because of me. Rejoice and be glad, because great is your reward in heaven . . ." (Matthew 5:11 NIV)

I was disappointed but not defeated. Campus Crusade was the only prospect I had, and until God showed me a different path, I had to pursue this opportunity. So, I wrote back to the Campus Crusade office in Nairobi to explain the situation and asked if there might be another way. I received a response from a man named Win Hurlburt, who told me not to worry; he would make arrangements for me. Soon thereafter I received instructions to go to the Air Burundi office and pick up an airline ticket. I could hardly believe it! I was really going to the conference in Kinshasa.

On the day of my departure, I went to the airport at Bujumbura, where I encountered the Burundi church delegation. "What are you doing here?" they demanded. "Are you going to Kinshasa?"

When I told them yes, they were incredulous. "But you don't have a recommendation from us."

I did not want to engage in this discussion because my going to Kinshasa had nothing to do with them. "Campus Crusade told me to come," I explained simply.

When we landed and deplaned in Kinshasa, I looked around for where I should go. Fortunately, I didn't have to go very far. A man I had never seen before rushed up to me. "Are you Mbanda?" he asked with a big smile. When I told him yes, he embraced me. Here was Win Hurlburt, the American who worked with Campus Crusade in Nairobi. At that moment, I felt an enormous relief.

"Let's go," Win said, leading the way to a large transport truck.

All the luggage and passengers, including the Burundi delegation, were being loaded into the back of the truck. I prepared to join them, until Win opened the passenger door to the cab and invited me in. I rode upfront between Win and the driver.

When we arrived at the center where the Campus Crusade conference was being held, I could tell by the looks on the faces of the Burundi delegation that they couldn't believe the red-carpet treatment I was receiving. While everybody was required to share a room, sometimes four people together, I was given private accommodations, with a fan—which was a very welcome given the heat in Kinshasa. I felt as if God had answered all the humiliations I had endured since returning to Burundi and had just "promoted me." I was so grateful.

As the conference got underway, my job was to interpret from English to French. After the first session, the Burundi delegation complained to the organizers, saying that I didn't understand French (I was fluent). The organizers replaced me for a session or two with someone from another delegation, but he said he could not understand American English. After that, the organizers brought me back as an interpreter and I worked the rest of that two-week conference. Nothing more was said about my language skills.

At the conclusion of the Campus Crusade conference in Kinshasa, I was supposed to go back to Burundi. However, Win Hurlburt asked if I would consider staying on with Campus Crusade and joining the team in Kinshasa as they started a center for training pastors and evangelists. Mine would be a multifaceted role as one of the trainers, as translator of materials from English into French, and as an administrator of the center. I was about twenty-five and eagerly agreed to this opportunity to officially launch my ministry career. Thus, what started out as a two-week assignment in Kinshasa turned into a role for eighteen months.

While I was working and living in Kinshasa, I was paid in U.S. dollars, about $200 a month. However, during that time Zairean currency devalued so much that it was possible to live on about $20 a month. After discussing the matter with Win, my boss, it was decided that I would be allotted enough of my pay to live on in Kinshasa and save the rest—accruing a financial nest egg for later on.

After my time was up in Kinshasa, I was sent to the Ivory Coast, in West Africa, where I worked for about six months. When that assignment was completed, Win asked me to travel with him back to Bujumbura, Burundi, to see how the office there was doing. Instead of progress, though, we found much infighting. Some of the staff and a couple of the advisory board members asked Win if I could be assigned there for a month to get the Burundi operation on track. Win was pleased. He wanted me in Burundi and to be a leader of the team, but was concerned about whether I would be accepted. Win made it my decision; I decided I would stay on and see what developed.

After Win left, things changed dramatically for the worse. The man who was in charge of the office had no interest in my experiences as a trainer or administrator. The Bujumbura office had a car, which created some tensions and rivalry around who was able to use it. This led to the idea that my role would be driver for the office. For the next three months, my job was to pick up the car in the morning, bring the team leader from his home to the office, and then collect the others. At midday I brought them home for lunch and then picked them up again, and at the end of the day, brought them back to their residences. Although I had to pick up and drop everybody morning, lunchtime, and evening, I was expected to leave the car at the office and walk or take a bus home.

One month turned into three months. When Win visited Bujumbura, he asked each staff member for a report on what had been accomplished. Everybody laughed when it was my turn, knowing that I had not been allowed to contribute to the plan.

"I've been the driver," I told Win and proceeded to give him a rundown of my daily responsibilities.

Win wasn't pleased. The car had caused infighting before and now he was determined to put a stop to it. "We are going to sell the Volkswagen and buy a small pickup truck that we can use for the ministry," Win said.

I raised my hand. "I'd like to buy this car." I had saved $500 and borrowed another $1,000 from a friend on a short-term basis until I could access the funds that were in my support account. Now, I had a car of my own, soon registered in my name. I nicknamed it "1221" after the license plate number: BU 1221. Even though at six-foot-five I was too big for the car, I loved it. (My wife, Chantal, tells me that back when we were dating, she used to love watching me get out of the car: left hand holding the top of the door, right hand still on the wheel, left leg out and trying to pull out the right. I suppose I did develop a sense of style.)

The next change Win made in the Burundi office was to have me take over as the country director for Campus Crusade. With Win's endorsement, everyone had to agree to my new position. I wanted to shout "Hallelujah!" finally feeling vindicated after being relegated to the lowest possible position in the office. For three months as driver, I kept quiet and observed, so I felt I knew what needed to be done to turn the ministry around.

In my meeting with Win, I tried hard to contain my excitement. I thanked Win and everyone for their trust to me. Then I went out for a good dinner with my friends; it was time to celebrate.

In Burundi, I worked with churches in the areas of evangelism, pastoral leadership, and discipleship. By this time, I was twenty-seven years old and had a staff of five. One of the requirements of the Campus Crusade model was for each person to undertake his own fundraising. In other words, each individual was expected to find support to pay his salary and other expenses. But in Burundi, this was a foreign concept, which Campus Crusade didn't fully consider. In addition, the church pastors in Burundi were largely unpaid and the churches had little or no money. Therefore, I changed the model for it to make sense for the local churches. We asked the churches for direct support for our missionary work, specifically for gasoline so we could drive to the villages, fuel to run the generator so we could show *The Jesus Film* (a 1979 film based on the Gospel of Luke that is widely used in evangelism), and meals and lodging for our staff when we were in the field. Church members were happy to collect for us and provide what we needed, sometimes in the form of money, but mostly with food people cooked themselves and lodging in someone's home. At the end of a three- or four-day visit, we would take a "love collection" in which people gave whatever they could—often chickens, goats, eggs, and bananas because they did not have money to spare. We sold these donations in the market and used the money for Campus Crusade operations. What Campus Crusade sent for operations was used for salaries.

While effective, this plan was technically in violation of Campus Crusade policies that money should be raised on the individual level, rather than ministry-wide. Furthermore, using Campus Crusade money for salaries was viewed as misuse of designated operations funds. Win did not see any problems with what I was doing; he thought I was being a creative problem-solver. However, I did get in trouble with the Africa Finance Director and the Director of Africa Affairs. Tensions escalated to the point that, in 1982, I was summoned along with Win to Campus Crusade headquarters in Arrowhead Springs, California, to meet with Bill Bright, founder of the organization, to explain what I was doing.

As far as I knew, the only reason I was being taken to the United States was to explain the funding situation. But, knowing Win, I suspected he would use this as an opportunity for me to tell stories about the ministry in Africa while he asked for funds. Together, we made a good team.

Although I was nervous about what might happen to me, I could not help but be excited to see the United States. This was an entirely different part of the world and I had no idea what to expect. The experience was overwhelming! Before this time, the most cosmopolitan place I had seen was Nairobi.

America was well beyond that; everything was modern and so big—the roads, the buildings, the crowds.

Our first stop was New York. I did not see much of it except the airport, which was very complicated with so many gates and travelers rushing here and there. From New York, we flew to California. From the airplane window I caught a glimpse of the vastness and beauty of the country—forests, cities, mountains, rivers, and an ocean on either coast. Win and I were there for only a few days, including a short meeting with Bill Bright. When I explained to him what I had done to change ministry support in Burundi, Bill told me, "I wish I had more people who were as ingenious as you are."

Then Bill reached for a copy of a *Living Bible* on his coffee table, wrote a few words in it, and signed his name. "God bless you in your ministry," he said, handing the Bible to me.

I was overwhelmed by this gesture, and felt blessed to be given this opportunity to work with Campus Crusade.

From California, Win and I went on to Phoenix, Arizona, where I spent three months, living with a family that was involved in fundraising for Campus Crusade. Soon, I became acquainted with two churches in Tempe, Arizona: Grace Community Church and Church of the Redeemer, where I met Pastor Vincent Strigas, who had visited Burundi and other parts of Africa. He knew of my work and had a keen interest in supporting me.

"With a little more education, you can do more," Pastor Strigas told me.

I was so inspired by his comment. He supported my ambition that I should further my education by getting a graduate degree. My daydreaming about the possibility of one day going to the States for an advanced degree was becoming a more serious plan. Every day, I prayed for God to show me the way to actualize the dream.

My three months in Arizona were transformational as I received more informal training and got to know more people. It was also fun and broadening personally as I visited the Grand Canyon, went fishing on a boat (I was still fearful enough to make sure I wasn't too near the edge), rode horses, and was introduced to an entirely different lifestyle. My family and friends knew I was in the United States, but where I was exactly and what I was experiencing was beyond their understanding. But for those who knew my ambition and witnessed where I had come from, it was nothing less than seeing a miracle unfold. In the States, as I met with people and explained my story, many of them struggled with the idea that I was without a home country. I was Rwandan by birth and identity, but could not go back to that country because of continued violence against Tutsis. I was a refugee in Burundi, but that country did not want me or my countrymen. I was stateless.

The two churches in Tempe were very interested in our mission in Burundi and raised money for us to do more, specifically to buy generators and two pickup trucks for our work in the field and to help support staff. Soon, it was time for me to return to Burundi. Before I left, though, one of my new friends in Arizona decided he was going to outfit me personally with almost a dozen of everything—pants, shirts, t-shirts, and more. Never had I been given so many new clothes.

I stepped off the plane in Bujumbura in style: blue jeans, western shirt, a cowboy hat, and cowboy boots. Plus, I had been given one more special gift: a Sony Walkman.

By this time, I had confided to Win my dream of going to graduate school in the United States. The more I talked about it with a few people who were close to me, the more real my dream became. But how to accomplish this? I would need sponsors, tuition, a place to stay. Yet, with all that had happened to me in my life, since I was a child fleeing Rwanda with my family, I had learned to wait for the Lord to show me the way. This recalled the words in Proverbs: "Trust in the Lord with all your heart and lean not on your own understanding; in all your ways submit to him, and he will make your paths straight" (Prov. 3:5-6 NIV).

When we talked about graduate school, Win saw a bigger picture for my life than simply my education. "If you are going to go to the States, it would be better if you are married." Win was thinking that if I went to the States as a single man, I might meet an American woman and not come back. Better to be married before I left Africa.

The idea certainly appealed to me. I was twenty-seven years old, a confident young man who had been to the States. No longer a ragged beggar, as I had been when I first arrived in Kenya, now I was a handsome young man driving around in a Volkswagen. I wore my western clothes and listened to American Christian and gospel music—the Bill Gaither Trio, Dallas Holm, and Kenny Rogers—on my Walkman. My favorite song was Dallas Holm's "He Knew Me Then."

It just so happened that across the street from where I lived was a family I had come to know. When there was a wedding in this family, they invited me to attend. I eagerly accepted.

As the preparations for the wedding party proceeded, I was at their house frequently. And, of course, I had my Sony Walkman with me, which drew the curiosity of some the younger members of the family, especially the kids. One of the young women in the group was tall and beautiful with an engaging smile. I found out her name was Chantal, the niece of the woman who lived across the street from me. I was determined to get introduced to her.

"What is that you're listening to?" the kids asked.

"Music," I replied.

They put their ear up to the headphones. "What kind of music is that?"

"American Christian music," I told them.

"That's Christian music?" They shook their heads.

"Yes, this is what they listen to in America."

All the kids wanted a turn listening.

"Nobody is going to listen to it, except that lady right there." I pointed to Chantal. She smiled and came over to me. I was so grateful for that Sony Walkman!

The day of the wedding, I transported some of the guests in my car. Among them was Chantal. As we talked, I learned that she, too, was Rwandan, but had been born in Burundi. Her parents had fled Rwanda about the same time as mine. The more we talked, the more a connection was made between us.

After the wedding, I told the aunt that I wanted to see Chantal again. She told me where Chantal and her family lived. Now I was a man on a mission.

Chantal's father owned a shoe store where Chantal also worked. The shop and their house were not too far from the Campus Crusade office. I passed by there at least twice a day, thinking of a plan to see Chantal, that tall, striking young woman with the beautiful smile.

Three close friends from the same church denomination and I had committed to hold each other accountable to our walk of faith—and to help each other find women of strong faith to marry. I had shared with them my meeting Chantal.

They could hardly wait to meet her for themselves and help me see her again.

We came up with a plan. We would go shoe shopping. Of course, none of us had any money for buying shoes, but, since my size was 13 or 14 wide, there was little danger of me needing to actually purchase something. No stores in Burundi carried my size. So I could look for shoes as a pretense, while introducing my friends to Chantal so they could tell me what they thought of her. At the store, we looked around and tried on some shoes, but, of course, nothing would fit me. Finally we struck up a conversation with Chantal.

After that meeting, my friends and I decided to invite her to church. It was very important that Chantal be a Christian because ministry was my way of life. I needed a life partner who could participate fully with me in my walk of faith and would come to trust in the Lord as much as I had learned to. After one of my friends talked to her, Chantal accepted Christ and started attending our church. Now our relationship could begin in earnest.

Although Chantal and I were both Rwandans, my background neither attracted nor impressed her family. Chantal's father was one of the most successful businessmen in the city. Her family did not know me, which in our culture was a real impediment. And, it wasn't enough to get to know me; they had to know my family tree! Fortunately, among Rwandans, and, especially among refugees, there were close connections. As it turned out, people on Chantal's mother's side knew of my family, although not very well. At least it was a start. On her father's side, there was some reticence toward me since they did not know my family. Both Chantal and I worked hard so that I would earn the family's respect. In the end, it was given, and I was embraced. The whole process took a little over a year. In December 1983, I proposed to Chantal. I had just turned twenty-eight, and she was twenty.

We married on April 14, 1984, in a beautiful ceremony at the cathedral, with a reception on the grounds with family and friends. It was very well attended—more than a thousand people—with amazing choirs and traditional Rwandan drummers and dancers. After the wedding celebration, both families hosted additional events, including a dinner for about eighty people at Club des Vacances, a resort hotel. As lovely as these celebrations were, all I could think about was how blessed I was to have found the "bone of my bones and flesh of my flesh" (Gen 2:23 NIV) named Chantal. We had each other (and for thirty-one years, as of this writing, we've been blessed in our marriage) and we were about to embark on the adventure of life together. Soon that journey would take us halfway around the world.

As we prepared to leave for the United States, we sold all our wedding gifts—anything to raise money. The proceeds, combined with the monetary gifts we received, amounted to about eight thousand dollars. Chantal and I were amazed. Never before had we seen so much money. "This is everything we need," I told Chantal excitedly. "We will have enough to go to the States and pay for your education and mine. Then we will come back."

On June 13, 1984, we left Burundi for the United States. Our families had mixed emotions—excitement that we were going to the States for education and sadness that we would be so far away from them. When they saw us off, most of them tried not to show their tears as they hugged and kissed us. Some of them held us very long, as if they would never let go. Friends kept urging me to go, while some of the women wanted to give Chantal one more hug.

Our ultimate destination was Pasadena, California, where I had been accepted for the summer term at Fuller Seminary. This had come about through the help of my friend and advocate Win Hurlburt, Dr. Paul Pearson, Dean of the School of World Missions at Fuller, and Dr. Charles Kraft, a cultural anthropology professor Win and I had met in Nairobi. Upon entering Fuller Seminary, I had to resign my position with Campus Crusade, but Win continued to help me with the resources to support Chantal and me while I was in graduate school. Plus, we had what we still thought was a lot of money—that eight thousand dollars, minus what we'd paid for our airline tickets.

We traveled from Bujumbura to Amsterdam, spending one night there in an airport hotel, and then flew to the United States. On our way to California, we made a side trip to Mesa, Arizona. Given my previous travel experience and prior visit to the United States and the fact that Chantal did not speak much English, I was the interpreter and storyteller. Chantal was overwhelmed by everything she saw: "Wow! Look at that! What is that? Did you see that?" Chantal had a good eye and admired many things, especially household items, which did not mean much to me at all. The difference in our tastes stemmed from the fact that she had been raised in a city with a family of means. I had spent so many years in a refugee settlement with almost nothing and was never exposed to such things. But we were both on a mission and were not going to be distracted by material things (even if we had had the means, which we didn't). Studies were on our minds.

In Mesa, we stopped at Church of the Redeemer to see Pastor Vincent Strigas, who, during my time there, had encouraged me to continue my education. "Everybody wants to see you," Pastor Strigas told us. "They have been praying for you since you left here. They will be so happy to learn that you've gotten married."

He asked us to stop by the church. Chantal put on a long Rwandan dress made of beautiful fabric and I wore a suit. Expecting to be introduced to church staff and may be some lay leaders, we went to the church office with Pastor Strigas. Suddenly, he changed his mind. "Rather than sit here, why don't we go over to the church building?" he said to us.

When we stopped in the multipurpose room, more than one hundred people from the church shouted "Surprise!" and "Welcome!" It became another wedding reception.

The outpouring was overwhelming, especially for Chantal, who could not understand most of the words being said to her. But the meaning was clear when everyone hugged her and gave us their best wishes. Then we sat down to a dinner.

Unbeknownst to us, Pastor Strigas had told the congregation that, if they were going to give us a gift, it should be monetary to help support us while I entered graduate school. These generous people showered us with money—more than two thousand dollars. It was a completely unexpected and unforgettable experience.

After the party, Pastor Strigas called me aside. Instead of taking Chantal with me to Pasadena right away, he suggested that she stay with him and his family for a couple of days. That way I could get everything ready for us in Pasadena—finding an apartment, registering for classes, and getting myself situated. We did just that, and, after a few days, Chantal said good-bye to her newfound American family and got on a plane to her new husband of two months. We could not wait to start the next phase of our life adventure together.

CHAPTER SIX

God's Zigzagging Road

"Where you go I will go, and where you stay
I will stay. Your people will be my people and
your God [will be] my God." (Ruth 1:16b NIV)

The Fuller Seminary School of World Missions campus in Pasadena was bigger than I expected, and busy with students who, like me, had come for summer school. I registered for my classes and paid for them from the money we'd brought from Burundi. Then I set about finding a place for us to stay. I was taken to an apartment; it was affordable but on the edge of a marginal area—a "little dicey" my friends called it. It was the best I could do with what we had.

The next day, a fellow student volunteered to drive me to the airport to pick up Chantal. Excitedly, I waited at baggage claim where we had agreed to meet, but Chantal was not there. I double-checked the arrival information; her flight had landed. Still no Chantal. Finally, there she was—happy to see me, yet clearly upset by her confusion in the airport.

Chantal tearfully explained that as she tried to make her way toward the airport terminal exit, the automatic doors caught her off guard. Expecting someone or something to come through them, she stepped back. The doors closed. She approached the doors again; they opened, and, reflexively, she stepped back. Chantal's dance with the automatic doors made her question the way out and, without knowing enough English, she couldn't ask anyone for help. Finally, she watched how other people were navigating the doors and decided to follow them. Scared of getting lost, she stayed with the crowd all the way to baggage claim where we were finally reunited. As we rushed to our friend's car, I was more grateful than ever for my brave, beautiful wife who had said yes to me, my ministry, and this adventure we were on.

Our new life was not going to be easy. Everything was expensive in California: tuition, books, our small apartment, food. The money we had expected to last for the two years of graduate school was going faster than we anticipated, just on our basic needs. Two things sustained us. First, our trust in the Lord. This did not mean that we or anyone could sit back and do nothing. As a hungry ten-year-old refugee boy, I had gone out with faith and intention when I found that pumpkin. Now we would have to go where the Lord led us to do his work, finding support along the way. We already knew from experience that God's path was usually a zigzag, comprised of unexpected twists and turns. Each setback or upheaval was an opportunity to affirm our faith and grow closer to the Lord. We would learn this lesson time and again.

The second thing we knew was the Lord leads us all into community with others. Never have I forgotten the people, often so poor themselves, who gave me food and shelter during my long trek to Kenya, and my relatives in Burundi, who took me in and gave to me from what little they had. In the States, we were adopted by the church community in

Mesa, Arizona. Now, in Pasadena, we had to put our trust in the Lord. Missionaries always have to raise support in the form of prayers and donations to carry out the Lord's work. Without a community behind us, we cannot minister to others—listening to their joys and sorrows, praying with them and for them, and sharing with them what little we might have. As I began this next phase of preparing for ministry and leadership, I recalled the words of Joshua: "As for me and my household, we will serve the Lord" (Joshua 24:15 NIV).

Given the short summer semester, the class schedule was compressed into long days: eight in the morning until four in the afternoon, five days a week. My first class was cultural anthropology, and the work was rigorous. For Chantal, it was also a long day, spent by herself in our small apartment. She only spoke a few words of English and didn't feel confident exploring on her own, especially since we were not living in a good area. Once, while Chantal was home alone, people kept knocking on the door. She didn't open it and was still very frightened when I came home that night. After that, we left together every morning and walked to the campus, where Chantal waited outside the classroom until lunch. We bought one hamburger and split it between the two of us. Then, after the afternoon class session, we walked home. This was our daily routine.

I registered for a second class, on church growth, and paid the tuition. With three months of rent paid in advance, our money was gone. Although neither of us complained to the other, we didn't have enough to eat.

Walking home from campus in the late afternoon, we passed a pizzeria. The smell coming from that open door made our mouths water and our stomachs rumble. We stood on the sidewalk, watching the pizza makers toss the dough in the air and catch it again. Chantal tugged on my hand; it was time to go home and make ourselves something small to eat.

My friend and former boss, Win Hurlburt, had assured me that support was coming from Campus Crusade, but that money was never released to pay my tuition at Fuller Seminary. Instead, Campus Crusade wanted me to go to the International School of Theology in Arrowhead Springs, California. That option did not interest me because it would be the same as what I had learned already. While at Fuller, I met other African students pursuing masters and doctoral degrees. We shared the same passion and vision for serving God back home in Africa, knowing our advanced education would prepare us to take on the leadership roles needed to carry out this vital and meaningful work.

The money didn't come from Campus Crusade, and Win, despite his best efforts, could not raise any funds for me. We had no choice but to leave Pasadena after three months, with four classes completed, and return to Pastor Vincent Strigas's house in Mesa, Arizona. We tried not to be discouraged by this setback, but did not know where to go next. We didn't have enough money to go back to Africa, and my student visa did not allow me to work. All we had were questions and no answers.

Then one day in early Fall 1984, Win visited Mesa as part of a fundraising trip to the States. Win had an idea: Denver Seminary in Colorado provided financial aid to international students. I was glad to hear his idea because I had already applied there and was awaiting a response. Even before I was accepted, Win arranged for Chantal and me to fly one way from Mesa to Denver where we were met at the airport by a friend of Win's named Lou Zier. Soon, Lou would become our dear friend as well.

Lou dropped us and our suitcases off at Denver Seminary, and we went to the admissions office. My application had been received, but I had not paid the thirty-dollar application fee. (A former missionary to Burundi who lived in the Denver area paid it for me.) Even though money was clearly going to be an issue, I was admitted on probation.

As we worked with administration, we met a woman named Joy Hesselbarth. When she learned we had come from Burundi and that I had worked with Campus Crusade, she told us excitedly, "My husband works for Campus Crusade. He would love to get to know you. Where are you staying?"

"We don't know yet," I answered. We did not have a place and knew nobody in Denver. It was another step into the unknown. For me, this was nothing new, but for my dear wife, it was quite scary.

Joy told us we could stay with her and her husband, Dennis; they had a room in the basement. We didn't know what a basement was, but we looked at each other and accepted the offer with a big smile and an excited "thank you." We stayed for three months, which was probably longer than they had expected. Never once did they make us feel anything but welcome. During that time Lou Zier and his wife, Bev, became good friends, inviting us to Southwest Baptist Church in Lakewood, Colorado. Two couples who were close to Lou took us to lunch after services and drove us back to Denver. Just as we experienced in Mesa with Pastor Strigas, there were other families willing to embrace us.

The next Sunday, when Lou took us to church, he made an incredible offer. "I have a pickup truck. I know you can drive. You can use it for as long as you need." He handed us the keys and we drove away with our own transportation to get to church on Sundays. Soon Chantal began volunteering at church in the nursery. The children loved her and she learned English from them.

Meanwhile, Denver Seminary gave me a scholarship equivalent to two-thirds of the tuition. To pay the remaining third, I got a job on campus, cleaning classrooms and bathrooms in the campus buildings. My work started at 5:00 p.m. and went well into the evening. Sometimes Chantal helped me and then we would walk the three miles from the seminary to our off-campus apartment

When Win came to Denver, he was so pleased to learn I was getting my master's degree. But he had one more item on his agenda. "It's very important that Chantal go to school," he said.

Chantal was eager to begin her own studies, but we had no money. Win was committed, though; we were both going to receive an education. True to his word, Win found funding so Chantal could begin attending Metro College in downtown Denver. We also had enough money for a security deposit and six months of rent for an apartment that cost $150 a month. Life was good and we were grateful, even though money continued to be tight. An anonymous donor from Lakewood began providing us with $75 per month for food and living expenses. To save money on gas, I didn't drive Lou's truck and walked the three miles each way to school instead.

When winter came, we were not prepared for the cold and snow, which was so foreign to us since Burundi and Rwanda are on the Equator. Even when we tried to wear layers, we weren't dressed warmly enough. A friend at the Seminary, Karry Kelly, stopped us one day. "Where are you coats?" he asked. "You need warm coats."

"We don't have any," we said.

There was nothing in the clothing donations that fit my

tall frame. Karry motioned for us to follow him. "Come on. I know where to go."

He drove us to Burlington Coat Factory. Just seeing those rows and rows of coats—long and short, wool and down-filled—we felt warmer. Karry handed me a big hooded parka with a fuzzy lining, and another for Chantal. It was hard to say whose smile was bigger: mine, Chantal's, or Karry's.

We were warm, but life in Denver still was not easy for us financially. We learned which churches had food pantries, what they handed out and when. We'd get a bag of rice from one church and cans of beans from another. "Guess what's for dinner?" my wife and I would joke with each other. One night we'd have beans and rice; then next we had rice and beans. On Fridays we got a treat: Cherry Hills Community Church gave out cheese and peanut butter—it was like Christmas!

Once a week, we walked to the grocery store to buy a cheap loaf of white bread and a jug of milk. Chantal's eyes trailed behind the women pushing carts heaping with food. They seemed like millionaires to us, buying whatever they wanted. We'd watch them cruise the aisles and wonder what they would do with so much stuff.

"One day," Chantal said to me tearfully as we walked home with our bread and milk, "I want to push one of those trolleys."

I took her hand in mine and squeezed it a little. "You will."

Instead of focusing on what we didn't have, we reminded ourselves every day of how blessed we were. The generosity of people who had embraced us, along with one anonymous donor, allowed us to live in Denver and attend school. I had wanted to pursue a master's of divinity, but that would take three years. A master's in Christian education was a two-year program, so that's what I pursued. It was important for me to get my diploma; I could always continue my education later.

One day, while driving to church in the pickup truck Lou had given us to use, I slowed down for a yellow light and prepared to stop. A huge truck hit us from behind, knocking our vehicle to the other side of the intersection. We were shaken up, but not badly hurt, although Chantal had bumped her head and her ankle was sore. I went to a pay phone to call Lou, who owned a small insurance company and knew exactly what to do. Within minutes, the police and a fire truck with paramedics arrived. Emergency lights blinked fiercely. It was more frightening then comforting to us.

Chantal was taken to a hospital near the seminary; the doctor wanted to do an X-ray.

"Are you expecting?" the emergency room nurse asked.

"No," I said.

"I don't know," Chantal said.

I looked at her.

"We'll give you a pregnancy test," the nurse said.

"That's a good idea," Chantal agreed.

My mind started to race: *We can't have a child now. We can't afford it. We have to wait. But Chantal wants a baby so much . . .*

The nurse brought us the results. "You're expecting."

The shock wave hit me: *We are going to be parents!*

Chantal beamed as she got off the examination table. "I'm fine. No reason to do any X-rays." As we went back to our apartment, the news began to sink in: The two of us were going to be three.

We had to find a doctor for Chantal and to deliver the baby. As a student, I had basic health insurance coverage for us, but it didn't cover maternity. We managed to find a doctor who charged us $900 for prenatal care and delivery. After Chantal confided to a couple of friends at church that she wanted to have one or two new things for the baby—a little outfit or fresh blanket instead of something used from the Salvation Army or the clothing collection—the church threw a baby shower with so many gifts, including a rocking chair. With her mother, aunts, and other family members so far away, Chantal felt blessed to be showered with love from these people who had adopted us.

When Chantal went into labor, everything started out according to plan. We waited until the contractions were close before leaving for the hospital. Then the contractions slowed. Finally, after many hours, our daughter Erica was delivered. But instead of taking our baby home with us after a few hours, Erica had a breathing problem and was taken immediately to neonatal intensive care. It broke our hearts to see our little girl hooked up to monitors instead of being held in our arms. The doctors advised us to leave the baby at the hospital and go home, since without Chantal in a patient room, the bill would be reduced. This was strange to us; in Africa, you do not leave your baby behind, you go home with your baby. The thought of leaving Erica behind brought us to tears. There was no way we could have done it, regardless of how much it cost.

When Erica was discharged, the bill amounted to more than $8,000. When we explained our situation, the hospital advised us to contact our embassy for assistance. "We are refugees," I told them. "We come from Burundi, but we are not Burundi citizens. We can't contact the Rwandan embassy, because they don't claim us either."

The hospital people were sympathetic, but they still

wanted to collect their money and expected us to make payment arrangements. But we had nothing with which to pay. Even the chairs in our apartment we had picked up from the curbs on trash day. As bills arrived at our apartment, we felt so bad; it had never been our intention to cheat or short-change the hospital or anyone else.

One day a letter came from a woman in Arizona. She had heard from our friends in Mesa what happened when Erica was born and knew that we were struggling. Inside the envelope was a check for $4,000. Immediately we brought that money to the hospital. They were shocked to see us and this money, because several months had passed. The hospital accepted the $4,000 payment and waived the rest. We were paid in full.

Then one day, while sitting outside of Denver Seminary, Chantal, who had stopped going to school because of money, was approached by a friendly woman who admired baby Erica. As they struck up a conversation, the woman introduced her-self as Alice Matthews, who did fundraising and marketing and reported directly to the president of Denver Seminary. Alice had lived in France and her husband had worked with the Conservative Baptist Church in the Ivory Coast.

"How are you managing?" Alice asked.

Chantal replied that we were doing fine. Sometimes things were tight, but somehow we got enough food and money to live month to month.

"This has to change," Alice said. "You can't keep living like this."

Alice went into the President's office and told the adminis-tration our story. Soon one third of the tuition was no longer my responsibility; the seminary covered the full cost of my education. My on-campus cleaning job could then be used for buying food and paying other expenses. We let ourselves dream about what would come next when I got my master's degree. By this time, Fuller Seminary had contacted me, inviting me back for summer school.

While I completed my M.A. in Christian Education from Denver Seminary, I had enough classes from Fuller to earn a second degree, either a master's in missions or in international culture. This also appealed to me because I wanted to enter the doctorate program at Fuller. There was one catch: I was not allowed to take my final exam to graduate and get my diploma because I had an outstanding tuition bill at Fuller. No matter that the Dean had authorized it, without payment, the registrar's office would not allow me to complete a master's from Fuller.

Here was another zigzag, a setback that disappointed, but in time built trust and bolstered faith. With a firm conviction that I had to continue my education, I spoke with Edgar Elliston, a Fuller Seminary professor who advised me to contact Dr. Ted Ward, who was in the process of moving from Michigan State to Trinity International University in Deerfield, Illinois. Ted advised and taught many African graduate and postgraduate students. When I contacted him, Ted encouraged me to apply to the doctoral program at Trinity. With the hope that I would be accepted, Chantal and I packed up our belongings and loaded one-year-old Erica into our old Honda Civic, which we had bought for less than $1,200 while we were in Denver. We drove straight from Pasadena to Arizona, where we stayed one night with friends, and then continued on to Deerfield without stopping for more than an hour to stretch our legs, take care of the baby, and get a little food.

Ted Ward was instrumental in my admission to Trinity, where I started in the doctoral program in the School of

Education. Our friend Pastor Strigas sent us $800 and promised to help us with our ongoing expenses. This was such wonderful news! Sadly, soon thereafter, Pastor Strigas died of a heart attack. We mourned the loss of our dear friend who had taken us into the community and embraced us like family. His loss affected us another way as well: His promise of support had been made verbally. With no written commitment, the church felt no obligation to continue our support. There I was again, trying to finish my education but without tuition money. At Trinity, I had not yet paid for my first quarter classes and could not register for the second quarter. We had no money for housing.

We confided our troubles to Ted Ward, who then shared our situation with the people of North Suburban Evangelical Free Church. Ruth McClellan, a woman in the congregation, spoke up: her home in Deerfield had a separate "in-law suite" where we could live. By this time, Chantal's sister Mediatrice had come to stay with us, so three adults and one baby moved into Ruth's home. The in-law suite in the basement was to be our space, but very soon Ruth and Chantal became good friends. Suddenly we were using Ruth's kitchen and then we were welcome to relax in the living room. Ruth literally opened her entire house to us.

What an amazing provision from the Lord! We were still receiving the anonymous $75 a month in support and another donor offered $25 a month. We could stretch that $100 for food, gasoline, diapers, and other necessities. When it came to my tuition, we kept praying for the Lord to show us a way.

One evening we received a call from our friend Lou Zier in Denver. "Is Chantal sitting down?" he asked me.

I knew this expression meant something unexpected had happened, which made me uneasy.

"Nothing is wrong," Lou assured me. "Get Chantal on the phone with you."

Sitting together, the telephone receiver between us, Chantal and I listened carefully.

"Someone has donated money to help you with school," Lou began. "I have the check here—for twenty thousand dollars!"

Twenty thousand dollars! I couldn't believe it. "Are you sure, Lou? How many zeroes are on the check?"

"Four zeroes," Lou laughed. "But there's just one catch: the person doesn't want to be known. It's only to be used for tuition and will be paid in installments directly to Trinity."

I let out a shout. "Hallelujah!" We called for Ruth to come and hear the news, and soon we were all laughing and crying and praising God. I never learned the identity of my secret benefactor and respected his or her wishes never to try to find out. But God knows, and I trust that this person has been richly blessed for such generosity without which I could not have continued my education or undertaken the work the Lord had for me to do. Once again, the words of the Psalm 121 echoed in my mind, just as it had on the long trek from Burundi to Kenya. "I lift up my eyes to the mountains—where does my help come from? My help comes from the Lord, the Maker of heaven and earth" (Psalm 121:1-2 NIV).

With my tuition paid, I was given a job on campus as a security guard. We later moved into a two-bedroom apartment on campus for married students. While at Trinity, our second child, Eric, was born in 1987.

Every day I studied hard and then worked as a security guard at night. Chantal took care of our two children and our little household. A church in Waukegan, Illinois, introduced Chantal to the Women, Infants, and Children (WIC) food and nutrition program, which helped support us. And so the Lord provided for our days at Trinity.

While I was there, my passport expired and had to be renewed. As a refugee, I had travel documents issued by the UNHCR. I made inquiries to the High Commissioner, but received no response; I had to do something. Ruth's daughter-in-law, Karen, who worked with World Vision in the refugee resettlement program near Toronto, suggested that we apply for "landed immigrant status" in Canada through the Canadian consulate. I approached the Canadian consulate in Chicago and they were kind enough to provide us information of how to approach our request. As we started the process, we filled out forms, submitted applications, and then waited for the documents to be processed. Karen worked on the other side of the border to make sure we had a church to receive us. The good news came after a few weeks of waiting. We were overjoyed with the possibility of someday having a citizenship, a country we would finally call home, and an end of our stateless status—though, spiritually, we knew our citizenship is in heaven.

The day came. We packed and moved to Canada, first to Guelph, Ontario, where a church community had agreed to sponsor us, and then to Quebec City, where we had some relatives and friends. After a short time in Quebec, I needed to get back to Trinity to continue my studies. Back at Trinity, when I shared with someone how my United States permanent resident "green card" application had been rejected, he challenged me to reintroduce it and to seek help if needed, because he believed the rejection was baseless. I reintroduced my application for a green card, and waited to see what would happen. During that time, though, I could not leave the United States, and Chantal, who was expecting our third child, could not leave Canada. We were apart for months.

Finally, with our documentation in order, and my family back with me in Chicago, I concentrated on finishing my dissertation, but was no longer considered matriculating full-time, so campus housing became more expensive.

I was offered a job with the International Students, Inc. (ISI), a ministry dedicated to outreach to international students, based in Colorado Springs. While the organization did not seem to be the right fit for me, we decided to stay in Denver near our support network, close to our friends and church community in Lakewood. I spent six months writing my dissertation, while working the only job I could find: delivering the *Denver Post* every morning. We tried hard to economize, but we were a family of four—and soon to be five. We owed a total of $675 in rent and had no way to pay it.

Pacing the floor of our small apartment, I prayed to find a way.

Chantal suggested that we call her father for help or one of our friends in Denver. But I couldn't do it. Instead, I encouraged us to pray.

"Do you think God is going to drop money out of the ceiling?" Chantal said through her tears.

As we prayed, I could only think of three possible answers: yes, no, and wait. I was waiting and wished I knew for how long.

There was a knock on the door. Erica, who was five years old, answered it. There was Bev Zier. "Mommy is in the bedroom," Erica told her innocently. "Daddy made her cry."

Bev heard the whole story. "Why didn't you tell us what was happening?"

The Ziers and the entire Lakewood church community

had done so much for us already, including presenting us with a second-hand Buick as a Christmas present the year before. (We had sold the old Honda, which had served us well, for $500 to another student.) We couldn't ask them for anything else.

A smile spread slowly across Bev's face as she laid three envelopes on the table. The first was a collection from the church for us: $675, coincidentally exactly the amount of money we owed in back rent. In the second envelope was $75 from the anonymous donor who continued to help us with living expenses. The third envelope contained $199 to the penny.

"Let me tell you about that money," Bev said. The Sunday school children had collected money—often nickels, dimes, and quarters—for two years with no adult donations. When the money was tallied, the children decided to give the entire amount to a missionary family. When asked who, they were unanimous: "Chantal and Mbanda!" They fondly remembered Chantal, their nursery school helper and English "student."

God had not "dropped money from the ceiling," but God did deliver it to the door! The next day, people from Lakewood brought so much food and groceries, our apartment was overflowing. "Never do this again," they told us. "If you have difficult times, you must let us know."

My prayer of thanksgiving recalled the words from Lamentations: "Because of the Lord's great love we are not consumed, for his compassions never fail. They are new every morning; great is your faithfulness" (Lamentations 3:22-23 NIV).

Finally, I finished my dissertation. I had been ordained an Anglican priest the year before. The dream I had as a poor refugee boy in Burundi had been fulfilled; the titles "Reverend" and "Doctor" now officially preceded my name. I recalled the words from the Chronicles: "But as for you, be strong and do not give up, for your work will be rewarded" (2 Chronicles 15:7 NIV).

In the circuitous ways of the Lord, with emotional highs and lows, I had learned deep lessons that extended beyond my coursework: The needs of the poor are more than material or financial; they are also emotional and spiritual. Yes, help for the hungry and needy must address the primary needs of food, clean water, clothing, and shelter. But feeding a body without tending to the spirit will not bring about true healing and wholeness. Each time our friends came to our aid, when that anonymous donor paid our tuition, when people brought food, they reminded us of the love of God. I would soon bring this first-hand knowledge into the fields of the Lord where I was being called to be a worker.

One day in March 1990, two months before my official graduation, while looking through a magazine, I read a job advertisement for an Africa director for the Christian Aid Mission. The job description called for someone with cross-cultural experience who could speak French and English; Swahili was considered a plus. "That's me!" I said excitedly.

I called the mission immediately and was put in touch with the President. "I read about the Africa director position and I think I am the person you are looking for," I told him. A few days later, I flew from Denver, where my family and I were living, to Dulles Airport in Washington, DC, and then to Charlottesville, Virginia, where Christian Aid Mission was headquartered.

"I got the job!" I told Chantal as soon as she picked up the phone.

She asked me the details of the assignment and how much

they would pay me. I had no idea. In my excitement, I forgot to ask about salary.

Sheepishly, I called the President's office. "I think there is something we forgot to discuss." They assured me that the salary and benefits were outlined in an offer letter coming to me by mail. Every day I waited anxiously, and finally, four days later, the letter arrived: I had a title and a salary. The Christian Aid Mission allowed me to postpone my start date until after our third child, Edwin, was born, and then we were off to Charlottesville, Virginia.

My salary of $29,900 sounded like so much, but with rent, car payment, and living expenses, the money evaporated. Life in the States continued to be more expensive (and complicated) than we anticipated. Our solution was for Chantal to find a job—any job that would bring in some money.

The President of the organization got wind of this and called me in his office. "I hear Chantal is working while you are traveling. What's going on?"

I explained that my salary couldn't keep up with our expenses. The President stopped me right there. "How much money is Chantal earning?"

I did a quick calculation and came up with about $12,000.

The President gave me note to take to the company's accountant, Bobbi. I handed her the note that said, "Give Mbanda a $12,000 raise."

Bobbi sighed. "Not again." Her smile told me the President had a habit of "redoing" budget items like salary without much formality. "At least this time he didn't write it on a napkin."

I spent nearly three years in that position, during which time Chantal launched a business buying used clothing in the States and selling them in Burundi. Chantal's father and one of his friends were our partners in the business, handling the logistics in the port in Kenya and the business in Burundi. The business grew quickly to the point where we rented a large warehouse, hired about twenty-five people, and had machinery for sorting and packing. We shipped about four to six containers a month to Africa.

Our share of the used-clothing business was enough to pay both Chantal and me a salary. I left Christian Aid Mission and worked full-time in the clothing business, which appealed to the entrepreneurial spirit I had developed as a young boy selling cigarettes, candy, and other small items. Although I did feel a little unsettled that I was spending so much time in business, Chantal and saw it as "tentmaking," meaning a way we could support ourselves while undertaking ministry. The term refers to the Apostle Paul, who was a tentmaker while also spreading the gospel (Acts 18:3 NIV). We tithed a portion of our earnings to establish the Christian African Leadership Ministry (CALM) to train others for service in Africa and to help people become more self-sufficient. (Today, this "tentmaking" model is called "business for missions.")

Then, one day, the bottom dropped out. Political upheaval in Kenya prevented our containers from leaving the States. Our shipments stacked up, and we lost more than $100,000 in fees and delays in shipping merchandise. We could not pay our suppliers on time.

As the business wound down in late 1992, I devoted time to prayer, asking God what was ahead for me. I did not have to wait long for an answer. One day the phone rang and, within hours, I was pursuing two jobs in ministry. Although they were with different organizations, they had one very interesting thing in common: No matter which job I pursued, we were going back to Africa.

CHAPTER SEVEN

The Call to Africa

*"He raises the poor from the dust and lifts the needy
from the ash heap." (Psalm 113:7 NIV)*

As our business wound down in Charlottesville, I needed to reexamine what I was doing and revisit my calling. One afternoon out of nowhere, the phone calls I received within an hour of each other made it clear that God had something else in mind for me and that Africa would be my destination.

The first opportunity I heard about was that the International Bible Society (IBS) was looking for an Africa director for French-speaking countries.

Within an hour, the phone rang again. This time it was Compassion International, which also was looking for an Africa director. I told them I was interested in knowing more and we agreed to continue our conversation. I reached out to one of my former professors at Trinity, who encouraged me to seriously consider Compassion International.

When I put down the phone, I couldn't quite believe what was happening. Within one hour I had received two calls about two job opportunities, both of them in Africa. God must be telling me something, because I felt calm and confident instead of restless as I had over the failure of our "tentmaking" venture. Later that day, Chantal and I prayed, asking God to show us the way to the next opportunity of His choosing.

Several weeks later I flew to Colorado Springs for an interview with IBS (now known as Biblica).

Then, at the hotel that evening, I passed someone I recognized in the corridor: Dan Brewster, who worked Compassion International, which was also based in Colorado Springs. When Dan asked me why I was in town, I explained I was interviewing with IBS. He looked surprised. "But we have been talking about you at Compassion. Come by for a visit if you can."

Since my sessions at IBS had ended early, I went back to the hotel and called Dan Brewster at Compassion International. He told me to come over as soon as possible.

I was impressed by what I saw at Compassion, how the organization functioned, and how organized it was. While I did like IBS's work of putting Bibles into the hands of people, Compassion International's mission touched me spiritually and emotionally. Compassion is dedicated to helping children, releasing them from poverty. The possibility of becoming Compassion's Africa director ignited in me a deep desire to serve the most vulnerable.

Compassion's work also brought me back to my own childhood in the refugee settlement, with the hunger and hardships I had known and experienced. This was the type of organization I needed when I was a child, but did not have. Visiting Compassion's headquarters, I could also see how they respected the dignity of the poor, in a way that I had not seen elsewhere. It was evident in the way they described their work and in the pictures in their offices. The poor are created in God's image. In the face of the hungry, the orphaned, the sick, the homeless, and the friendless, we see a reflection of the Creator. These are the precious ones about whom Jesus spoke when he said, "Let the little children come to me, and do not hinder them, for the kingdom of heaven belongs to such as these" (Matthew 19:14 NIV).

As I left Colorado Springs, I wondered what God was doing. These were two very good organizations, both looking to send someone to Africa. One was about to make me an offer, while Compassion International had an opening, but had made no such offer (I hadn't even had a formal interview). As I reflected, I could not deny the leaning in my heart. No matter what happened next, I wanted to stay in touch with Compassion International. But it would be up to the Lord to lead me where I could be of most service.

In the end, I was offered a job with Compassion International. Suddenly, everything in my life made sense, all the way back to the refugee camp, when I was starving and found a pumpkin in the jungle.

Now that Compassion was moving forward, I had another round of meetings. The last one would be with Ed Delgado, an American who was Compassion's Africa director, based in Nairobi. After several years in that post, Ed wanted to come back to the States; I would be his replacement.

Then, the unexpected happened. Compassion called to say Ed had decided to stay on as Africa director in Nairobi. But there were two other positions: a program coordinator in Haiti and a program development specialist working with Ed in Nairobi. The choice was easy for me: I loved Compassion, I had a heart for Africa, and the program specialist job entailed program design and implementation, which I loved to do. All it lacked were line management responsibilities, which

I hoped to take on in time. Beyond all this, Compassion would bring me into the ministry of uplifting children in poverty.

In January 1993, I officially accepted Compassion International's offer, with a start date of March 15. I left for Nairobi where, among other things, I would see the Compassion field office. Being back in what I once considered the hustle and bustle of a contemporary city was surreal. As my colleague Ed and I drove around, I remembered what it had been like when I first entered this city—alone, penniless, and without any idea of how my dream of an education would be fulfilled. I recalled the hours I spent on the corner looking at the Hotel Ambassadeur and the terrifying night I spent in a Kenyan jail because of mistaken identity. Now, I was a well-educated program development specialist.

I was living in two worlds. With my United States green card, which I had finally been granted, I was part of the international community of expatriates, Americans and Europeans. These were the type of people I had seen at the Ambassadeur, sipping coffee and eating well. But I knew the other side, too, of being a refugee, hungry and homeless. Never would I lose my humility and forget that it was the Lord who had brought me to this point in my life—transformed and ready to serve.

When I returned to Charlottesville, Chantal and I packed up our household, selling what we could. Then we went out to Colorado Springs for orientation. There was much to learn, but I grasped it eagerly. The headquarters were smaller then than they are today, probably less than a hundred people were there at the time. I'm a natural networker, so I quickly met everyone. By June 1993, we were ready—Chantal and I, with our three young children—to leave for Nairobi.

After our long flight, we were so happy to see a familiar face greeting us: Ed Delgado, who had come with some of the Compassion staff to meet us. We were taken to a guest house in Nairobi near the office. I arranged for a vehicle and rented a four-bedroom house. With these amenities arranged, I could not wait to dive into work. There were many challenges facing us in Africa. The Democratic Republic of Congo, the largest country in Africa in terms of land mass, was in political turmoil. We also had started working in Ethiopia, which had been torn by political uprising and devastated by drought and famine.

Nearby, in Rwanda, after a civil war and a very tenuous peace agreement, tensions were still simmering. Although I was so grateful to be a permanent resident of the United States, I was still Rwandan. From the time of my childhood, there had been ethnic pogroms in Rwanda against the Tutsi. It has been estimated that as many as 150,000 Tutsi fled Rwanda in the first waves of violence in the late 1950s and early 1960s. Those who fled became refugees in other countries: Burundi, Tanzania, Kenya, Uganda, and other places as well, including Europe and North America. Many young Rwandan men in Uganda joined the Ugandan army. As they came together and received training, they formed a group known as the Rwandan Patriotic Front (RPF), which would become a global network of refugees, exiles, and their supporters. Among the RPF leaders was a tall, thin man trained by the Ugandan army and later in America, named Paul Kagame, who much later would become Rwanda's President, a role he continues to hold as of this writing. He has been an amazing leader—exactly what Rwanda has needed.

I had become aware of the RPF in 1988 when the Rwandan diaspora met in Washington, DC, and I attended as part of the community of Rwandans living outside our homeland. A number of the RPF cadre were at that gathering, and I heard their plan that, one day, it would be possible to repatriate all Rwandans. As time went on, it became clear that plan would never materialize as long as Rwanda's president at the time, Juvenal Habyarimana, remained in power.

In October 1990, the RPF launched its first incursion from Uganda into Rwanda to challenge Habyarimana's regime. At first, the RPF troops were overwhelmed and, under the command of Major General Paul Kagame, retreated into the Virunga Mountains to regroup and retrain. By the end of 1991, the RPF controlled a larger area along Rwanda's northern border, which it shares with Uganda and the Democratic Republic of Congo. The RPF's headquarters was at the Mulindi tea plantation, in northern Rwanda.

By 1992, Habyarimana came under international pressure to legalize opposition parties, which meant negotiating with the RPF. But there were extreme factions within Rwanda's political landscape, including a virulent group that spewed ethnic violence and hate-filled propaganda. By July 1992, peace talks began in Arusha, Tanzania, between the Habyarimana regime and the RPF. On August 4, 1993, the Arusha Accords were signed—a peace agreement between the Rwandan government and the RPF—ending a three-year civil war. By September 1993, the United Nations established the United Nations Assistance Mission to Rwanda (UNAMIR) and sent troops to the country as observers and peacekeepers.

Despite the peace agreement and the presence of the United Nations, Rwanda seemed as tense and volatile as ever. In addition to U.N. troops, French soldiers had been dispatched to Rwanda to support the Habyarimana regime. Although the international community refused to acknowledge it at the time, escalating violence against Tutsis was already raising the specter of genocide. Making it more dangerous for Tutsis in

Rwanda was the presence of extremists in the Rwandan government. Feeling threatened, people who could flee left the country, but had to do so secretly to avoid arrest under suspicion of being loyal to the RPF.

While all this was happening, I was sitting in an office in Nairobi, underutilized in my new position. My immediate supervisor was talking about going back to the States. He was so distracted that he couldn't orient me in my assignment or deploy me to develop programs. I did what I could to make myself useful: I studied Compassion's policies and field manuals. I literally read them cover to cover, memorizing entire sections of them. I knew every Compassion program and could quote policy to the letter.

Ethiopia was under my direction, as we recruited and trained program staff there. Compassion International had a very small operation in Rwanda, and, with the Arusha Accords in effect, we decided it would be a good time to undertake program evaluations there, to see the work Compassion was doing and decide whether it could be expanded. Rwanda was my responsibility, which meant I had to do a field visit. I hadn't seen my country since I was five years old. I was about to make my journey home.

When I landed in Kigali, the capital city of Rwanda, I could barely get off the plane. Sweat poured off me. An American colleague, Gordon Mullenix, who had lived in Africa, knew what was happening. He literally led me through the airport, which was being patrolled by French soldiers, and helped me fill out the immigration card. At Rwandan immigration, I wondered if I would be found out—if my name, Mbanda, would trigger some recognition. I was named after a chief in my village whose name was Mbanda and who had been a target in the first wave of massacres. Would anyone remember him and associate me with him? Would I be arrested for that alone?

Gordon picked up our baggage, and we stepped out of the airport into a sea of travelers and those meeting them. Compassion's country director in Rwanda was a Rwandan named Simeon Pierre, but I was not ready to begin speaking to him in our native language, Kinyarwanda. I did not want to draw attention to myself.

By the time I reached our hotel, Chez Lando, I had convinced myself I would be killed; someone would burst in my room and shoot me or else plant an explosive device under my bed. At the hotel, I recognized a man named Karenzi, who was a member of the RPF. I did not know him, but had seen his picture. Seeing him gave me peace of mind. If the RPF was at the hotel, then I was safe.

The next morning, we went to the Compassion International office, where we were greeted by the staff. Gordon and I introduced ourselves and shared devotions with them. But some people in the office approached me privately and asked, "Why are you here? Don't you see how dangerous this country is?"

I told them that our plan was to visit about ten program sites in Rwanda and so that's what I was determined to do. We headed north to Gisengi. We passed through two road blocks patrolled by high-ranking soldiers loyal to the Rwandan army of the Habyarimana regime. I barely breathed as they asked the driver and the passenger in the front for their documents, fearing I would be singled out. But they never asked for documents from the three of us sitting in the back and waved our car on.

When we arrived at Gisgeni, we checked into the Palm Beach Hotel. Suddenly I heard my name being called. "Mbanda!" A wave of fear rolled over me and nearly dragged me under. Then I saw him: Abidjah, who had been one of my trainees at the Campus Crusade in Kinshasa. When he hugged me, he could feel my fear rising and see the sweat that slicked my face.

"Nobody can touch you!" he said loudly.

I tried to quiet him down; being discreet seemed prudent. But Abidjah assured me I was safe, as he knew high-ranking officials in the Habyarimana government. In Gisengi, we visited several church-based education and nutrition programs for children, but my fear was so great, my heart just wasn't in it. Then we returned to the hotel. Abidjah came to see me, inviting me out for dinner, but I didn't want to leave the hotel. Finally, I decided that I was probably safer with him than anyplace else. So, I went to his house to dine with him, his wife, and children, and two other people, a director for Compassion International and Gordon. There were moments like this when I could relax, but soon my fears returned.

The next day, we headed south to Butare. A woman I knew back in Burundi, a distant relative of mine, lived in that town. She and her husband had moved back to Rwanda after studying in Burundi. Her name was Christina Bakamana. I asked at the hotel if anyone knew her and was told Christina worked at the bank. Our driver took me to the bank where I asked for her. As Christina approached, I could see her expression of alarm, even though she was fighting to appear calm.

"Don't tell me you are here," she whispered as she hugged me. "They are going to kill you." She was fearful for me because I was coming from the outside and could be suspected of being associated with the RPF.

I stayed only a few minutes at the bank. Christina asked me where I was staying. "This evening," she said, "maybe my husband and I can visit you."

As I left the bank, my fear returned, stronger than ever. This was not an irrational thought in my head. Christina had expressed what I feared ever since I got off the plane from Nairobi.

We traveled next toward the Burundi border to visit a Baptist church that had a Compassion-sponsored program for children. As we toured the site, Simeon Pierre, the country director, asked me about my family's home in Rwanda. I told him we came from Runyinya— that's where my grandfather was born. Then I told him the family name; he recognized it.

"My parents were from Nshuli," I continued. "My father was a teacher there."

"We are not far from there," Simeon told me. "It's just over there." He pointed to the Shororo Mountains in the distance. That was exactly where my parents' house had been.

"Can we go there?" I asked, suddenly wanting to see my family's homeland—the place my father had come from, the place where I was born. My childhood memories were vague, and now I wanted to reconnect with the place we had been forced to leave when I was only a small boy. After hearing all the stories over the years, it seemed important, even though there was danger on these roads, to claim this connection.

We went together, Gordon, Simeon, the driver, and I. At Nshuli, we stopped at the school where my father had taught. Immediately I was struck by how few trees there were compared to the lush forests I was told about as a child. The banana plantations were still there, but were not as well kept up as I remembered my grandparents' grove. I spoke to someone, inquiring about a teacher named Evariste. Evariste was dead, I was told, but his son was a teacher. When I met the son, I explained that our fathers had been friends, and told him my father's name, Martin Rwangoga.

"My parents talked about him—and the cows he had," the man said excitedly.

I entered a time warp as I walked into that school and saw the classroom where my father had taught. As a little boy I thought of that school as being so big, but it was small with few classrooms.

My parents' house was gone, but someone from my father's family remained in the area: my grandfather's brother—my great uncle.

He was an old man, unable to see very far or hear very well. When I approached him, he seemed confused. Then I got very close to him and spoke my name loudly.

A look of recognition crossed his face. He took his walking stick and pushed it into my stomach. "I see your height. I see your father's face," he told me. Then he hit me on the hip with the stick. "Go! I don't want to see you killed in my face."

My great-aunt, refused to even look at me. I got back into the car and left.

We returned to Kigali and then left for Nairobi. When the plane touched down in Nairobi, I raised my hands in the air and said, "Thank you, Lord." I went home and told Chantal everything. "I don't know what I was thinking. I could have been killed."

Back in Nairobi and our safe life, I kept thanking God that I was alive. Some of my colleagues thought I was brave and some held suspicions that I was somehow connected with the RPF. But in my own mind, I was only foolish, not thinking about my family or what would have happened to them if I were killed.

The news out of Rwanda escalated in severity. Tensions were heightening. The Arusha Accords were not holding and, by March 1994, violence gripped the country. Then, on the night of April 7, 1994, I got a call from a friend in Nairobi telling me President Habyarimana had been killed, his plane shot out of the sky. Later, it was learned that the plane was shot down by Rwanda extremists who were plotting the genocide and thought Habyarimana was too weak to carry out their despicable plan.

At the time, we did not know what the President's death meant. Would it open the door for political change and an opportunity for real peace? Nor did we know that Habyarimana's assassination was a signal to start the genocide against the Tutsi. By the end of the next hundred days of horror, dubbed the 100 Days of Slaughter, approximately one million people would be massacred, including my great uncle and his wife.

It had been decided months before that, on April 8, I would travel to Bogota, Colombia, for a Compassion International meeting. We flew to the States; first to Atlanta and then to Miami, before heading to Bogota. At the airport, the terror in Rwanda was in the news everywhere. When I passed through American immigration, people offered their sympathy for what was happening in Rwanda.

The meeting was supposed to start on April 9, but I wouldn't be in Bogota for long. Compassion's head office urged my colleague Dan Brewster and me to go to Colorado Springs to figure out an action plan for relief and humanitarian aid for Rwanda. We needed to assess the needs in Rwanda where mass killings were leaving tens of thousands children orphaned and countless traumatized people. We also needed to learn about Compassion's office in Rwanda. The RPF was on the march, making its way from the north to Kigali, the capital, in the center of the country. With the U.N. powerless to intervene and the West refusing to act, the only way for the genocide to stop was for the RPF to be victorious.

Before leaving, I met with Compassion International President Wess Stafford. "Whatever needs to be done, do it," he told me. "And when you go, don't go empty-handed."

With that, despite grave personal danger, I prepared to return to Rwanda.

CHAPTER EIGHT

Into the Horror

*"So do not fear, for I am with you; do not be
dismayed, for I am your God. I will strengthen
and help you; I will uphold you with my
righteous right hand." (Isaiah 41:10 NIV)*

Dead, dying, wounded, orphaned, traumatized. This describes Rwanda in April 1994, as genocide swept across my tiny home country. By the time it was over, in early July 1994, the dead would number as many as one million. One million people in three months.

What many people did not realize was that the travesty committed in 1994 had actually begun thirty-five years earlier—with "practice genocides." It has been estimated that 200,000 Tutsis fled Rwanda in the first waves of violence in 1959–60, among them my family and me, and that as many as 20,000 were killed. By 1964, more than 300,000 had left the country.

As Compassion International prepared to respond to the crisis in Rwanda, I flew to Nairobi and spent a short time there to help organize our initial relief effort. Remembering what Wess Stafford had told me, we were not going in empty-handed, merely to be "observers." We would bring whatever relief we could: blankets, water containers, and nonperishable food. Our focus was always on the children, but given the extreme nature of the situation, we would help whomever and wherever we could.

Our plan was to fly to Kampala, Uganda, and then drive six to seven hours down to the Rwandan border. Upon our arrival at the border, however, we were met with complete chaos, with many nongovernmental organizations (NGOs) there. The big relief organizations were there, such as World Vision, Save the Children, and CARE. There were also some "briefcase NGOs," as we called them: people who came just to check things out. They took pictures so they could go home, raise funds, and talk about the problem. Among that vast sea of people were also journalists and others who had just come to see what was going on.

On the Rwandan side we saw a few Rwandan Patriotic Front (RPF) soldiers and some people dressed as civilians who were serving as immigration officers. They asked us who we were and what we intended to do in Rwanda.

I recognized one of the immigration officers; I had known him back in the refugee camp in Burundi. When I spoke to him, he acknowledged me, but maintained a business-like composure. He was military and didn't want to appear too friendly toward me.

At the checkpoints I greeted people, sometimes in Kin-yarwanda, sometimes in Swahili, and sometimes in English (Uganda, where many of the RPF came from, is English-speak-ing). My colleagues joked with me: "Everybody knows Mbanda!" The remark was good-natured, especially coming from my American and Ugandan colleagues. The other per-son with us was a Compassion volunteer from Canada; I'll call him Gilbert. When he said, "Everybody knows Mbanda," there was hostility in his voice.

We were allowed to proceed and soon passed the area of the Mulindi tea plantations, where the RPF was headquartered. It was green and lush, in places as dense as a forest. But the atmosphere was tense and focused. We went a little deeper to the town of Byumba, which was also controlled by the RPF. Here we encountered the first large group of displaced people, who had escaped the fighting and murderous bands of the *interahamwe,* a paramilitary group trained to carry out terror and mass killings and to incite violence among the people.

Byumba, like so many of the towns we first entered, had been "carved up" by the NGOs. Some were quite possessive about it and did not welcome another NGO on "their" turf— mainly, I think, because of fundraising and wanting to appear as if they were the ones doing the most work. I took our team to see the RPF representative in charge of displaced persons: Dennis Karera, a tough military man with a gentle spirit. He was the most humble soldier we met, willing to listen to everybody.

When we entered the first refugee camp, we saw the evidence of what evil can do: the ravages of body, mind, and spirit. People were in rags, many of them bone-thin, but with swollen feet and legs from having run so far and for so long. Some bore the deep gashes on their heads and limbs from machete wounds. It was almost too much to see, and yet we did not close our eyes. I was aware of my colleagues watching me. Among the initial relief staff, I was the only Rwandan who had been a refugee. When they asked me, "How are you feeling?" I assured them I was okay. Ever since we left Kabale, Gilbert had become more vocal about his opinions— often anti-RPF. When we were securing trucks in Uganda, he said he didn't want to rent from a Rwandan refugee. As we pushed deeper into the country, I had to wonder why Gilbert had come. He had lived in Rwanda a few years earlier and had volunteered for this mission. But was he really interested in helping victims? Or did he have some personal or political agenda? Based on his comments and the questions he asked, I began to suspect Gilbert's sympathies lay with the Habyarimana regime.

We distributed blankets, water, rice, and beans, but there were so many NGOs there, we were tripping over each other. After a whole day in Byumba, we did an assessment of where we could be most effective. There were so many lost, frightened, wounded, and orphaned children.

Given our primary mission of serving children, we wanted to make sure we gave special attention to the youngest victims who were on their own, those who had become separated from their families and needed someone to care for them.

Compassion headquarters had arranged for two containers of medical supplies to be shipped to our staging area in Uganda, as well as truckloads of relief supplies, such as food, water, blankets, and soap to take into the country.

When we returned to Kabale, word got around the NGOs that I was Rwandan, which led some to assume I knew more than I did. Rumors were rampant and many looked to me to get the news on how the RPF was doing: Was it a strong army? Were they also killing people? Did they really want one Rwanda or were they out for revenge? I could not tell them any more than what they had heard.

When the supplies were arranged, we left Kabale and went back into Rwanda to continue our assessment of need, identifying areas where we could safely establish relief outposts and distribute supplies. As we handed out food, water, and blankets, I felt fulfilled. These were my people and this was my home country. But it was bigger than that. I felt deeply that I was fulfilling my mission, the work I believed God had called me to do. The words of Jesus, from one of his parables, applied directly to our work, and I took heart from them: "For I was hungry and you gave me something to eat, I was thirsty and you gave me something to drink, I was a stranger and you invited me in, I needed clothes and you clothed me, I was sick and you looked after me . . . Truly I tell you whatever you did for one of the least of these brothers and sisters of mine, you did for me" (Matthew 25:34-36, 40 NIV).

On this rescue mission, I found myself, once again, living in two worlds—as a Rwandan refugee and a leader of an international relief convoy. On the one hand, I identified with the victims of the violence, never forgetting that I had once been a hungry, scared child, on the run from deadly violence. On the other, I was part of a rescue mission, attending to physical needs where we could and always remembering the spiritual need for comfort and solace.

To keep from becoming overwhelmed, I focused on the work at hand. There was so much to do and the needs were so great. Everywhere in these makeshift camps for the displaced were countless sick, wounded, and dying people. Children had deep cuts and gashes that crawled with flies. Mothers held nearly lifeless babies.

I came upon a man one day, seated alone on the ground, his head in his hands. I tried to talk to him. "I'm the only one who survived," he told me. When I looked in his eyes to pray with him, I saw the depth of his torment.

For two days, we administered relief in Byumba, returning each night to Kabale. There, we loaded up with more supplies and pushed deeper into the country. Our plan was to go to Gahini and then on to Kibugu in the east-central part of Rwanda. With our RPF escort, we traveled the side roads, sometimes needing to turn around and retreat very quickly because of fighting up ahead. In these moments, I felt the most danger. The RPF controlled the area, but the forces loyal to the existing government and the *interahamwe* still roamed the countryside. If they should find us, I would be in danger. My documents identified me as an American, but I could be recognized as Rwandan. I impressed upon my colleagues that should we ever be stopped by hostile forces, they had to say I was an American. If they identified me as Rwandan, I would be killed.

I looked Gilbert in the eye when I said that. "And if you say I'm Rwandan, I'll tell them you are Belgian." The reference was crude on my part, perhaps, because several Belgian soldiers had been brutally murdered at the start of the killings. But I needed to impress upon Gilbert that this was not the time for his comments.

As we drove along one road, we passed a convoy of RPF. From the brusque and efficient manner of these soldiers, we surmised that one of their leaders was with them. They let us pass and we continued down the road. Suddenly, we saw more soldiers up ahead. Because of the convoy we had just seen, we assumed they were RPF, but couldn't be sure. Why was there a roadblock here? The *interahamwe* were notorious for their roadblock strategy. They would stop people trying to flee and demand to see their government ID cards, which marked whether someone was Tutsi or Hutu. Anyone who was a Tutsi was attacked and killed.

The soldiers approached our vehicle. One of them came to the passenger side where I sat. When I saw his face, I recognized him: Lieutenant Colonel Jackson Rwahama. I had met him in Burundi after I graduated from Kenyan Highlands.

When I taught English in Burundi to support myself, Jackson had joined me as a teacher. His serious facial expression changed into a smile when he saw me. I saw the gold in his teeth: It was Jackson.

Instantly, I relaxed. Until I let my guard down, I hadn't realized how terrified I had been. I got out of the truck, and Jackson hugged me. When I explained our mission with Compassion, Jackson told me the area was safe. Soon we were on our way.

As we drove, the mood inside the truck changed. Although I couldn't exactly say why, I could tell my North American colleagues had reached the conclusion that I was highly connected with the RPF and had come to Rwanda primarily for political reasons, not the humanitarian mission. No matter how much I explained that I had known these people years ago—that they, like me, were refugees in Burundi, Uganda, Congo, Tanzania, and so on and that we had friends in common—I could tell that Gilbert, especially, preferred to believe his own theories.

Along the road from Byumba to Gahini we passed banana plantations and sorghum fields, all unharvested because the people had been killed or had fled. The most chilling sight were the stray dogs that looked fat and lazy. We could only assume the horrible truth of what they had been feeding on.

When we arrived at Gahini, we went directly to an Anglican church that I had visited during my field visit in 1993. Connected to the church was a health center. At this compound, there was a cadre of RPF who were teaching people about their philosophy, particularly "one Rwanda for all Rwandans." This was crucial to the nation-building that would later take place, to begin the reconciliation and unification of Rwanda, which continues to this day.

The RPF acted so kindly toward the local people and to

us as we offered supplies at the church and the health center. Gilbert, however, kept up his cynicism and suspicion. "These people are cunning," he said of the RPF. No matter that the RPF was on a mission to stop the genocide, Gilbert seemed convinced that the RPF only wanted power and was not concerned about the local people.

Now the truth of Gilbert's agenda was clear. He had not come to help, but to see for himself whether the RPF was the liberating force it claimed to be or was it a dangerous mercenary army. He was clearly the wrong person to be on this assessment and rescue mission. He was not alone. Later we met other NGO volunteers who, even as they helped the people, were vocally anti-RPF.

After this, when I spoke to the RPF and local people, I became guarded with what I shared with my colleagues. I told them the essential information: where we would be safe, how far we could go, where displaced people were being gathered. But some things I had to keep to myself, mostly because of Gilbert and my fear that he could compromise our mission with his political comments.

All along the road from Gahini to Kibungo, in east-central Rwanda, we could see signs of fresh fighting. Bundles of belongings lay by the side of the road, where people dropped what they were carrying and ran. Machetes and spears littered the ground and sometimes we saw bodies.

We passed two vacant vehicles, parked at the side of the road, and then a little church to the left. We pulled over and got out to see if anyone was there. As we approached the church, the silence was terrifying, as if a pall had been draped over it. We pushed open the door and stepped inside. The walls were sprayed with blood, and bodies lay everywhere. From the way people fell and the wounds on their bodies, it appeared they had been killed by both machetes and automatic guns. The bodies and the blood were still fresh; this massacre had happened only hours before.

It was more that we could bear. Although I was an ordained Anglican priest, there was nothing I could do for the hundreds of dead people, fallen like broken branches on the ground. My colleagues were visibly shaken and talked among themselves about how horrible it was. I was silent. As I got back in the vehicle, no words formed in my mind or on my lips. I had nothing inside me except bitterness and anger that this most egregious of crimes was being carried out systematically against innocent men, women, and children.

The *interahamwe,* drunk on violence and with lust for blood, came into a small village with the sole purpose of carrying out the massacre and inciting neighbors to kill neighbors. People, seeking safety, ran to the church, because in the past that had meant sanctuary. But not this time. Later we would hear many reports of people running to churches, only to be mowed down by machine gun fire or grenades. The bloodbath at the church was, tragically, only one of countless other scenes of violence and desecration.

At Kibungo, the town had been all but destroyed by fighting. The presence of the RPF made us feel a little safer, but we were aware of danger all around us; this area was only newly secured. We went to where displaced people had been taken and provided some relief as we undertook an assessment. The work was soothing, giving me a place to focus other than on the horrific scenes burned into my mind.

As we conducted the assessment, we were always looking for children who were orphaned or separated from their families. We gathered them together and tried to find a safe place for them. We were doing the equivalent of triage; whenever we found an older person who could take in children, we placed children with them and provided relief supplies to support them.

I continued that relief work for months, operating between Kabale and the centers we set up in Byumba, Gahini, Kibungo, and later Kayonza. We moved right behind the advancing RPF forces, identifying areas where we could set up stations to distribute relief and care, especially for children. We were moving from north to south.

On our third trip with supplies out of Kabale, as we were coming back from Kinbungo to Byumba, we saw an RPF convoy on the side of the road and had to stop. One of the soldiers leaned in the window and asked if Gilbert was in the car.

Gilbert, who was driving, identified himself.

The soldier smiled. "Welcome to Rwanda, sir." He waved us on.

I did not let on, but I recognized that soldier from the meeting of the diaspora in Washington in 1988. As we pulled ahead, I noticed this soldier talking on his radio. A short distance down the road, we were stopped again. A soldier approached the car and asked if Gilbert was with us.

"Yes. I am Gilbert," he replied.

Again, the soldier just smiled. "Welcome to Rwanda, sir." Without ever being threatening or even sarcastic, they wanted Gilbert to know they'd heard about him, his political views, and his disdain for Rwandans (such as his refusal to rent trucks from anyone who was a Rwandan refugee).

This time Gilbert's eyes were on me. Clearly he thought I had put them up to it, but I had not.

Again another roadblock and again the same exchange, always ending with a smile and the same phrase, "Welcome to Rwanda, sir."

By the time we returned to Kabale, Gilbert was fuming. He called me aside. "Did anyone ask you about me?"

"No," I told him truthfully. "This was the first time I ever heard them ask for you."

After that, though, Gilbert had enough. Feeling uncomfortable and unwanted, he packed his bags and left for Kampala, Uganda. Where he went from there, I do not know.

Sometimes, on the weekends, I would return to Kabale and then travel back to Kampala, where I would fly to Nairobi to spend one night with my family. Being back with them felt like medicine for my weary spirit. Chantal and the children were so worried about me and what was happening in Rwanda. Erica and Eric, who were nine and eight respectively, asked questions I found hard to answer. They wanted to know about the killings, who the perpetrators were and who the victims were. What did Tutsi and Hutu mean and which group did our family belong to? I tried to shelter them from what was happening, but they heard so much in the community and in the media.

Edwin, who was four, asked me, "Daddy, what can we do to help?"

The innocence and sincerity of his question touched me deeply. "We have to pray," I told him. "Daddy goes to help those who need it."

When I left Nairobi, I knew my family was praying for me and for the victims. Their prayers sustained me through very troubling times, when I saw so much human agony. I would think of Edwin's face and know that, even in the midst of unfathomable suffering, God hears our prayers.

I kept up a rigorous schedule, only going home every few

weekends and then for just a day or two. Others took longer R&R—four or five days in Mombasa, Kenya. I do not begrudge them any of that time to restore themselves. But I could not be anywhere except where I was: in the midst of the suffering of my people.

At the front lines of Compassion International's relief response, we were right behind the RPF as the liberating forces advanced toward Kigali. When they reached the capital city, the corrupt regime fled. The RPF took over the government and started the long, difficult process of restoring order and rebuilding a failed nation. It would take until 2000 for Rwanda to get on its feet and then another decade to made progress socially, economically, and politically, all building on a national platform of forgiveness and unification: one Rwanda for all Rwandans.

Kigali was a ghost town. So many people had been killed or fled. The Rwandan government has estimated that, at the end of the genocide, an estimated 75 percent of the Tutsi population inside Rwanda had been killed. I couldn't imagine that the beautiful city would one day be restored. There was no electricity, no water, and very little food. Into this vacuum of destruction poured millions of refugees, from Burundi, Tanzania, Kenya, and elsewhere; they had been waiting for the moment when they could return to their country. (As of July 1994, there was an estimated 3.5 million Rwandan refugees; by 2011, only 70,000 were still living outside the country.)

As the refugees flooded in, they took over any house or dwelling they could find to shelter themselves. It was chaos. Poverty, hunger, and fear spread like a plague. A nauseous smell hung in the air—the odor of death and decay. None of us wanted to eat or drink, but we forced ourselves. Many relief people were near exhaustion or pushed beyond their physical and emotional limits. My Compassion colleagues and I reminded each other that we had to eat. Sleep was another problem. People encouraged each other to be healthy and to see to their own emotional needs.

We set up our base in the Compassion International office in Kigali. Fortunately, much of it was still intact. We cleaned it up, restored a functioning office as best we could (electricity was available only a few hours a day), and set up guest quarters for ourselves. From that base, we could distribute relief supplies, while also embarking on other important work: tracing children in the country who were being helped through Compassion's donor network of sponsors. The radio stations were operating again. Before and during the genocide, radio broadcasts had been used to spread corrosive propaganda to incite violence against the Tutsi. Now, radio was used to disseminate information and to help calm the people. I was interviewed on the radio to give an overview of what Compassion was doing and to seek help for finding lost children. With so many people displaced and killed, it was very difficult. We started by identifying the churches that Compassion worked with and contacted them, hoping to find that the pastor was still alive. When there was no one at the church, we looked for survivors from that village who could tell us what happened to families.

Word got out among our network. Pastors who survived contacted us with information and requests for assistance. On our many field missions, we gathered displaced and orphaned children and arranged for care.

As supplies were trucked in from Uganda, we arranged for warehouses and had them secured to prevent looting. The initial chain we had established worked: supplies were dropped at Byumba, Gahini, Kibungo, and Kayonza, and then brought to Kigali.

The second week of July, we went to Kibungo, to visit one of the centers for displaced people and a home we had established for orphaned and unaccompanied children. As we drove along mostly unpaved roads, I noticed two people talking outside of a small house. I yelled for the driver to stop the car. He slammed on the brakes.

I ran toward the two people, one of whom was a woman. She saw me and screamed. I threw my arms around her and held her so tightly that I actually lifted her off the ground.

It was my mother. I had not seen her in four years.

The others came out of the car to see what was happening and began taking pictures of this unexpected mother-and-son reunion. My mother told me how she had come back to a refugee camp in Rwanda with a group of people from Burundi. She said that someone she'd met had a radio and had heard something about Dr. Laurent Mbanda attending to people and providing relief at the camps for the displaced. "I told them, 'That sounds like my son.' But when did you become a doctor?"

My mother knew I was in school, but understood that I was in the ministry. "I have a doctorate degree," I explained.

"What kind of a doctor? I have a bad headache."

"No, Mom," I said, trying to explain the kind of "doctor" I was. "I am a Ph.D. I have a doctorate in philosophy."

She looked at me, puzzled.

"That's the kind of doctor that doesn't help patients."

My mother explained the whereabouts of my four sisters and two brothers (including François, who was with the RPF). The team left me with my mother so I could see my four sisters and some of my nieces and nephews, who I had never met, and went on to Kibungo town center and then returned for me on the way back. We gave my mother a few of our relief supplies and then made our way back to Kigali.

Our work finding the children who had sponsors intensified. The sponsors, most of whom lived in the United States, were contacting Compassion's home office, trying to find out anything about the children they sponsored. Were they still alive? Were they sick or hurt? Compassion sent us names and we set out to find them. Every child found was a cause for celebration. We knew that prayers were coming our way from the head office, from church sponsors, and from the sponsors. We could almost feel that benevolent force behind us as we went about our work.

From Kigali, I could go home to Nairobi on the weekends. Sometimes I would get a ride on a U.N. cargo plane on Friday or Saturday and return Sunday night or Monday morning. I also brought Chantal and my children with me on a trip through Uganda to Byumba (I was not yet ready to take them into Kigali). There, they could see the relief work being done by Compassion and actually participate in handling out supplies to displaced children. I wanted to instill in my children a sense of service and the importance of taking care of others. Although they have all followed different careers, I know this was a formative experience for all three.

As the Program Development Specialist based in Nairobi, I had responsibilities beyond the Rwandan relief work. Like everyone, I was spread pretty thin and tried to hire staff to help us. Looking ahead, I knew we had to change the nature of our mission from relief to rehabilitation and so I developed a timeline of when that should be accomplished.

Finally, I put a strong team in place in Rwanda, including a new country director. Having replaced myself on the ground in Rwanda, and, with staff in place to carry out the Compassion mission, I was able to move back to Nairobi in December 1994.

By early 1995, it was clear that Nairobi had changed. When the RPF captured Kigali, the forces that were loyal to the former regime fled to other countries, including Kenya. Rising tensions were palpable and Rwandans were often targets. One day, as Chantal and a group of other women left a church, they were verbally accosted by a group of men. One of them rushed the women and tried to steal a purse from one of them. The men, we later learned, were personal bodyguards for Agathe Habyarimana, the widow of the former president whose plane was shot down. Mrs. Habyariamana was said to be part of an extremist faction in Rwanda. Shaken by the incident, Chantal and her friends ran to their car and drove home. Nairobi wasn't safe for us anymore.

In late May 1995, my family and I returned to the States, going to Colorado Springs for furlough. By this time, we had been in Nairobi for two years. While in Colorado Springs, I was sent by Compassion to a counseling center according to the protocol for anyone who was doing challenging field work overseas. In addition to their questions about how I was feeling, the counselors needed to determined whether I was grieving and needed counseling for that. I assured them I was doing okay.

Chantal and I then met with the HR department at Compassion's headquarters. When they asked me if I wanted to go back to Kenya, I answered affirmatively without hesitation. I wanted to be involved in Rwanda and the region as a whole.

Then they asked Chantal, "Do you feel safe?"

She hesitated, looked at me warily, and answered. "Nairobi is not safe for us."

CHAPTER NINE

Returning to Africa

". . . He will give you rest from all your enemies
around you so that you will live in safety."
(Deut. 12:10 NIV)

I was torn. In the end, we chose safety over heading back to Nairobi, and while I was grateful that my family was safe, away from any threats to our lives and well-being, my heart remained in Africa.

Staying in Colorado Springs forced me to embrace the unexpected. All I had known up to this time was Africa, but now my job would be to evaluate Compassion International's programs in Latin America and Asia, which led me to travel to such places as Indonesia, Thailand, the Philippines, India, and Brazil. Being involved in that side of the world helped me develop a global perspective on Compassion's programs. Coupled with the fact that I had first-hand experience with what it was like to be a child in need, I became one of the few people in the organization who fully understood all aspects of Compassion's work and had observed it first-hand in the field.

In June 1996, I was promoted to program director, responsible for all its field offices across the globe. This new position sparked a journey of leadership and led to a number of promotions until, in 1997, I became Vice President for Program Development, a position that required me to travel worldwide, including back to Africa. In 1998, while in Nairobi for a conference, I saw the church leader who, years before when I was fresh out of Kenya Highlands Bible College, had refused to recommend me for the Mweya school teaching position or the Campus Crusade job. For years, I resented the Burundi church delegation—and especially this man. Now it was time for me to come clean about the negative feelings I had been harboring.

"Would you forgive me for the bitterness in my heart?" I asked him.

The man extended his hand. "I knew it would work out for you. That's why I did it."

I was shocked that he could convince himself he had been trying to build my character or increase my faith by purposefully keeping me from an opportunity.

"No," I told him. "You did not know how things would turn out for me. You are not God."

I was deflated by the experience, but felt at peace. I had done what I needed to do by letting go of my bitterness toward this man. I did feel some sadness that we could not embrace as brothers in faith. But I am not God, either, and I cannot say what work is being done in this man's life. All we can do is accept our own lessons and do the best we can with what God provides.

During the late 1990s and into the 2000s, my family and I settled into a comfortable life. We were living in beautiful Monument, Colorado, where we had bought two and a half acres of land and built a house. Our children attended schools in the best district in Colorado Springs. We were living the American dream!

As content as we were, we never clung to that life. It's not that we feared it would be taken away; God has always provided for us, even in our most dire time. We lived without focusing on material things, but on the richness of love, friendships, family, education, and opportunities to serve, and, in doing so, we have experienced the words of Jesus: "I have come that they may have life, and have it to the full" (John 10:10 NIV).

But a full life in the Lord is often one of change. Even when we bought the land in Colorado, we prayed that we would never become so attached to it that we would resist hearing God's call to go somewhere else. We put down roots, but allowed ourselves to be "transplanted."

The change began with a family trip back to Africa in Summer 2003, just as our daughter Erica was preparing to go off to college that fall. It had been eight years since we left Nairobi. Since that time, much healing had occurred in our home country—politically, socially, emotionally, and economically. With more of our immediate and extended family living in Rwanda, we wanted to go back and visit everyone.

When our children left, they were nine, seven, and four; now, as young adults, they were experiencing Africa from an entirely different perspective. When we landed in Nairobi, the first question Eric and Edwin asked was, "Is this Africa?" This cosmopolitan city didn't look anything like they had expected. As I took them around Kenya, to see the different places I had lived and to Kericho, where I had gone to school, they absorbed everything: Kenya Highlands Bible College, the dormitory where I stayed, even the library where

I studied. Before leaving Kenya, we took a three-day safari, which completely enchanted them with the natural beauty of Africa. I had grown into a nature admirer, as well, and, seeing my family enjoying the experience made me enjoy it all the more. From the safety of the tourist jeep, I could relax into the wonder and beauty. And, I had a to chuckle seeing myself as a tourist, partaking of what had been available only to others before.

The children kept asking us, "Why aren't we living here? Why aren't we in Africa?"

In Rwanda, as we drove around meeting family and friends, the children saw the rebuilding of the country. In the capital city of Kigali, the skyline was coming to life with new construction: hotels, restaurants, and office buildings. The countryside was still agrarian, but the "thousand hills" of Rwanda were more beautiful as the country was peaceful and growing again—lush green and terraced into small farm lots for raising bananas, beans, maize, and other crops. Even more compelling was the spirit of the Rwandese people, determined to overcome the brutality of the past and to move forward toward a future of unification and reconciliation. In churches and elsewhere in the communities, we encountered people who spoke with hope and pride for the leadership of their country and the bright future that now seemed possible.

One night, at our hotel in Kigali, Chantal and I found our children conspiring. "We've been thinking," they told us and then presented their plan. "Aren't you supposed to be helping the poor? Then why don't you move back here and help them?" the children took turns inquiring. They wanted to be a part of Rwanda's revitalization—everything from building a hotel to opening an ice cream shop. Chantal and I just listened, impressed by their vision and passion, and not wanting to say anything that would dampen their youthful enthusiasm. "If you lived here, you could be so much closer to the poor people you're trying to help."

These were the same questions I had asked myself countless times, ever since I entered missionary work. How could I bring help and hope to those in need? How could I reach out, especially to the children who were as I had been—hungry and without a secure future? Here, too, were the words of St. James—the very definition of service—urging us all to "look after orphans and widows in their distress . . ." (James 1:27 NIV). My own children were ready to leave behind our comfortable life in the United States in order to take up a life of greater purpose.

"I would come back here, too," Chantal assured me. "We can sell the house in Colorado and move here."

I kept quiet, not wanting to respond right away until I had discerned this calling. The next morning at breakfast, my family confronted me. "We're all talking about coming back to Africa, but you haven't said anything as yet."

"Yes," I told them. "We can move back." The moment I articulated that thought, I felt peace settle over me like a warm blanket. As we prayed together, in the quietness of my soul, I felt God had called us back to Rwanda.

After that, I wrote an email to the Chief Operating Officer of Compassion, copying my immediate supervisor. "When I come back, I want to talk to you, as a brother in the Lord and as my boss."

Soon thereafter I received a response from my supervisor, who said he was willing to listen, but confided, "I'm not sure I like where this is going."

In August, we returned to Colorado Springs, where I met

with my immediate supervisor. Starting the conversation was hard, but the truth was easy to say: "I think I am resigning from Compassion International to go back to Rwanda."

For a few days, I tried to meet with Wess Stafford, President of Compassion, but it appeared to me that he was avoiding me, not wanting to hear from me directly what had been hinted about through the upper ranks of the organization. Then Wess invited me to have lunch with him in his office. When I announced my intention to resign, he seemed shocked. He challenged me with questions, such as security for the children in Rwanda, uprooting them from life in America, given their ages and years in school. In response, I explained the call I felt to return to Africa and that my current job as Vice President of Program Development was a global position. Leaving Compassion was the only way I could see to do what the Lord intended for me in this next phase of my life and more specifically in Rwanda.

Wess asked me several questions: "Have you prayed about this?" Yes, I told him, and related briefly how I had given this idea prayerful consideration.

His next question was more pointed: "Are you going into politics?" His question was logical given that elections were underway in Rwanda. Several members of Parliament were up for election, and even President Paul Kagame, the major general who had led the Rwanda Patriotic Front (RPF) forces to victory to end the genocide, was up for re-election. "No," I assured him. "I have no interest in political life." To silence any concern or speculation around this, I made my resignation effective December 2003, two months after elections would be completed.

Wess then asked me if God had said no—meaning, did I feel any disquiet around my decision. In fact, it had been just the opposite: The more I thought about going back to Rwanda, the calmer and clearer I felt about the decision. Finally, he asked if Chantal and our children were supportive. "Yes," I told him. "They were the ones to approach me with the idea before I said anything to them."

At this, Wess clasped his hands together. "Then I will release you. But Compassion International is your home. Anytime you want to come back, you just let us know." He promised to stay in touch with me frequently. By this point, we were both in tears.

Chantal and I were very touched when Wess reached out to Erica, who was staying behind to attend college in Alamosa, Colorado, to assure her that he would be there for her when she needed someone.

Once a week, the Compassion leadership team had what we called "executive chapel," a mid-week service that was led by each Vice President in turn. I used the next executive chapel service to read my resignation letter that I had carefully crafted. When I finished it, Wess and the other Compassion leaders came to the podium to embrace me. As we prayed together, there were tears in every eye, including mine.

For the next two months, I devoted myself to a smooth handover to my successor. Of all the leadership lessons I have learned in my career, transitions and successions are among the most important and the ultimate responsibility of every leader. When transitions are ineffective, it's not just the individuals who suffer, but also the entire organization.

My travel was more limited during this time of transition, but I did need to visit some of the field operations to ensure that they felt informed and supported. These field visits also allowed me to say good-bye to people who had become very close to me as colleagues and also brothers and sisters in the Lord.

But the sweetest good-bye of all was in late October when Chantal organized a surprise birthday party for me. I had recently returned from a trip to Latin America. Chantal sent me out for some errands and, when I came back home, more than sixty of my closest colleagues and their families were in our house. As they shouted "Happy Birthday!" I felt the shock of just how loved and embraced I was by these people.

As everyone left that evening after a wonderful celebration, I had my first real case of "cold feet." What were we doing, going off like this? Compassion was our family! I hadn't even left and already I felt lonely for my friends and colleagues. Yet, my mind was made up. I felt secure in the decision that God was calling us back to Africa. I could not let anything dissuade me from the plan. Then a few days later, my son, Eric, asked me a very simple and seemingly obvious question: "Daddy, when you go to Rwanda, what are you going to be doing?"

Suddenly, I felt the impact of my decision. I had no job there and no means to support myself. Thanks in large part to all the moving expenses, I didn't have the means to buy our airplane tickets. Erica was enrolled in college in the United States, but Eric and Edwin were coming with Chantal and me. While, in hindsight, it might seem rather naïve of me not to have considered this before, I had become so swept up in the conviction that I needed to go back to Africa, I hadn't given much thought to the logistics and other practical matters like having a job.

"I'm sorry, Daddy," Eric apologized, seeing the look of shock on my face. "I didn't mean to upset you."

Before I had time to say much to him, Eric ran off to catch the school bus.

The rest of the day that question gnawed at me. As I had at every other major juncture in my life, I had to rely on the Lord to provide. While that was relatively easy when I was a young man back in Burundi with no money or possessions, my life had become more complicated. I was a husband and a father now, with a good income, a house, and all the life considerations that go with that.

I sought the advice of a friend, Charlie Dokomo, at Compassion International, telling him my dilemma: "I'm committed to go to Rwanda, but I don't have a job."

Charlie immediately told me he had friends at other Christian nonprofit organizations and offered to let them know I was available. Within three days, I had three offers: two in Africa (specifically Mozambique and Senegal) and one in Chicago. Later on, another group approached me about a position, based in Kansas, which focused on Africa.

As I pondered what I should do next, my son Eric offered to help me with my decision. "Think about language, culture, Christianity, and the family, Dad." Clearly the Lord was using my son as part of my discernment process. When I thought about Eric's four criteria, it seemed obvious that I needed to focus on Rwanda, which was the intersection of language, culture, religion, and the family for me. Thus confirmed in my conviction to focus on Rwanda and East-Central Africa, I would have to turn down all four of those offers.

When I went into the office that day, David Dahlin, who was then the Chief Operating Officer of Compassion asked to meet with me. "If we could find a position for you in Africa, would you stay?"

"Yes," I told him, "provided that it would take me to Rwanda."

Then David smiled and nodded. "We might have something for you."

For some time, Compassion had been thinking about starting a program that would address HIV/AIDS and its impact on children. A donor had given money to fund the initiative and, given my background in program development, I seemed to be a likely candidate.

Quickly, a round of conversations ensued, the result of which was my being offered a new position with Compassion International, developing an HIV/AIDS curriculum. As we discussed the program, though, it clearly made the most sense from a programmatic perspective to be based in Nairobi. Our family would be in East Africa, which would allow us to visit Rwanda frequently and easily. In addition, Nairobi had excellent American schools for Eric and Edwin, which Rwanda did not have at that time.

Living and working in Kenya, I could never forget my first experiences there, and always thought back on the woman selling corn in the market who gave me food eat and seventeen shillings for the bus fare. On an earlier trip to Kenya in 1991, I had gone back to that market in Ahero and told this story to give testimony to the graciousness of God who provides for us in our hour of need and in hopes that someone would speak up and say that they remembered her or knew her name. But no one ever mentioned her to me.

Operating out of Nairobi, where Compassion had more of its program resources, the HIV/AIDS curriculum could target an urgent global problem that was having a devastating impact in Africa among all segments of the population, including children.

According to a 2003 report from the Joint United Nations Programme on HIV/AIDS (UNAIDS) and the World Health Organization, the HIV virus had spread across sub-Saharan Africa in the late 1970s. By the early 1980s, the epidemic stretched from West Africa to the Indian Ocean. By 2003, an estimated 5 million people in South Africa were living with HIV/AIDS. Botswana and Swaziland had the highest prevalence rates, at 38 percent and 33 percent, respectively.*

As the program director for the HIV/AIDS curriculum, I was assuming a lesser position and receiving a smaller salary than when I was a Vice President at Compassion's headquarters. But this was immaterial to me. Here was meaningful work to be done on behalf of the most vulnerable population—poor children in Africa, including those with HIV/AIDS, and those at risk of contracting the disease later in life. That this was what the Lord intended for me at this stage in my life was without question.

In early January 2004, just a few months after our family trip, we were going back to Africa—this time to stay. The hardest part was leaving Erica behind to attend college. But she, too, was strong in her faith and confident in the Lord's provision. As she later reflected, "As close as our family is, one would think that this would have been a tough decision, but it wasn't. The Lord had been preparing for our family for a while, and in that moment, when we made the family decision, I had so much peace in my heart, I knew that I would be okay."

---

*UNAIDS and World Health Organization. (2003). *Quality and Coverage of HIV Sentinel Surveillance: With a Brief History of the HIV/AIDS Epidemic.*

Working closely with the Compassion team in Africa and back in Colorado Springs we worked hard to deliver an effective curriculum that first year. The rollout was successful and, by the end of the first year, we were joined by a new team member, Scott Todd, who took over the HIV/AIDS program. By the end of 2004, I had transitioned out of my role of directly running the HIV/AIDS program and was reassigned within the Africa team. The director for East Africa was promoted to become director for all of Africa. I became the associate to the Africa director, focusing on East Africa.

Shortly after this transition, the Africa director expressed his desire to retire and began his transition to become a consultant to Compassion. At that point, I took over responsibility for all of Africa. By now it was early 2005, and security in Kenya had become a serious issue due to a rash of break-ins and carjackings. With growing instability in the country, Compassion began looking for a new location for its Africa office. Among the places we examined were South Africa, Zambia, and Ethiopia, as well as Tanzania and Rwanda. Any personal preferences I may have had did not weigh into the decision at all. Instead, Compassion leadership looked at several factors, especially security for the international (expatriate) and local staff members, communication, education for children, easy travel in and out of the country, tax issues and more.

After thorough study, the conclusion was Rwanda. Although it did not meet all the criteria, the potential of the country outweighed every drawback. Rwanda, with the government's ambitious "Vision 2020" plan to transform the country, had embarked on a turnaround that won the praise of many in the international community. The Rwandan government was welcoming to Compassion, and its zero tolerance for corruption made the country an excellent place for us to do business with the government and other NGOs.

In Rwanda, Compassion found a country on the rise. And I, of course, found the homecoming I had longed for back in 2003. Without any lobbying or manipulation on my part at all, the Lord had brought me from Nairobi into Rwanda to continue to do the work God intended for me.

If there is a lesson for anyone to learn from my experience, I share it here: Whatever you feel the Lord calling you to do should not give you any anxiety. You may not know how it will unfold; in fact, you should be prepared to be challenged and surprised along the way, for that is part of the growth process. But if this desire is truly aligned with what God's will is for you in your life, you have nothing to fear. God is never in a rush to bring things to fruition, but He is never late. Trust in the Lord and all will be well. This is the essence of how Jesus taught the disciples to pray in what has come to be known as the Lord's Prayer: ". . . your kingdom come, your will be done, on earth as it is in heaven" (Matthew 6:10 NIV).

Now it was nearly twenty-five years later, and Compassion had deep roots in Kenya. Wrapping up our operations in Kenya was not easy; Compassion had been active there since the early 1980s. With respect for the laws of the country and with good stewardship of our operations and staff, we moved from Kenya to Rwanda. Compassion's new Africa office in Kigali was in the new Tele 10 Building, which was part of the modern construction after the genocide. It was also quite close to the Rwandan Parliament building, which, for anyone who has visited Kigali, is an impressive landmark, but not for the reasons that most people think about government buildings. The Parliament building still bears the pockmarks of shelling from the last days of fighting between the Rwandan Patriotic Front (RPF) and the former government regime. To this day, those "scars" are visible as a reminder of what was endured by the country and its people to put an end to the genocide and the corrupt regime that left behind a shattered nation—but could not kill the Rwandan spirit.

Rwanda was an exciting place to be in the mid-2000s, a place of optimism and vibrancy. Compassion was undergoing its own growth and transformation, as we were expanding, especially in West Africa, adding Ghana and Togo to our operation in Burkina Faso. In East Africa, our operations spanned Rwanda, Kenya, Uganda, Ethiopia, and Tanzania. I was promoted back to the vice-president level, as Compassion organized into regional offices for Latin America, Asia, and Africa, each led by a vice president. Unlike my colleagues who headed their regions from the United States—the Asia vice president in Colorado Springs and the Latin America vice president in Miami—I wanted to stay in Rwanda. I was so firm in this conviction, I was not sure if that would disqualify me from becoming a candidate for a regional leadership position. The decision was made to try the geographic arrangement for a year, which must have worked well, because we never discussed an alternative.

Because Rwanda had no American school, we had to find arrangements for our sons' education. Eric was in Grade 11 and wanted to go back to Monument, Colorado, for his senior year and to graduate with his former classmates. He lived with a family we knew in Colorado to finish his secondary education. Edwin, who we call Eddie, was accepted into the Black Forest Academy, a Christian boarding school in

Germany. With Erica in college already, Chantal and I were alone in Kigali. For both of us, though, it was a time to grow in ministry and a love of serving God's children.

For me, my time as vice president for Africa was one of the most rewarding. Compassion's work in Africa grew to serve more than 500,000 children in East and West Africa, with over 400 staff members and a network of numerous churches. Our focus was on the holistic needs of children—spiritually, intellectually, physically, and socially. Although Compassion is not a community development program, we did address such issues as potable water, access to medical facilities, and other physical and social needs to improve the living conditions of children and their families. (This was done through what we called the Compassion Complementary Development Fund.) In addition, when a disaster occurred, whether on a national or local level, Compassion had the resources to step in with assistance.

With our own three children grown and in school in the United States and Europe, Chantal had time and energy to devote to others. In Rwanda, her maternal love found a wonderful outlet in a ministry she established in 2006: New Hope Home. There, orphaned and abandoned children were provided the same love and care that parents would provide to their own children. Often the children came to us through the police, the Red Cross, or community members who found unattended children. Some had been abandoned and left to die; instead, they found new life at New Hope Home.

This was twelve years after the genocide, but the traumatic effects of the violence left deep wounds among so many people. Traumatized children grew in age but not in the ability to care for themselves or others; as a result, there were teenagers having babies who didn't want them and couldn't care for them. I remember one young girl who brought her infant to New Hope Home, but, when she finished school, came back for her child. This was the rare exception. Most of the New Hope children had no one who loved, cared for, or spoke for them. And into that void stepped Chantal with her maternal heart and passion to take in these children.

New Hope Home started with ten children who lived in a house where they were cared for by several "aunties" (women volunteers); the ratio was one adult to two children. Even more important than the physical care, housing, food, and education these children receive is the love that is lavished on them. Love truly is the greatest gift one human can give to another; for children, being loved and knowing they are wanted, is essential to their development. As Paul wrote to the Corinthians some two thousand years ago, "And now these three remain: faith, hope and love. But the greatest of these is love" (1 Cor. 12:13 NIV).

Initially we funded New Hope Home ourselves. I would come home from the Compassion office to find that we no longer had curtains on the windows or that our television set was gone, because Chantal had brought these things to the New Hope Home. Later on, when we expanded to thirty children and three houses in Kigali, Chantal traveled to the States to undertake fundraising. Many were the times we "prayed" in respect to funds—asking God to lead Chantal to donors who would open their hearts to the needs of these children. Many people were very gracious and supportive of her work. In the early years of New Hope Home, when Rwanda allowed international adoptions, four of these children were adopted by loving and caring families in the United States.

As of this writing, we have twenty-eight children, ranging in age from six to sixteen. We have since sold the three houses in Kigali and built one large, comfortable home in Musanze, in northern Rwanda, where we now live. No new children have come to New Hope because of a change in government policy, which favors placing children with foster families and encouraging local adoptions.

We have loved and cared for the New Hope children as if they were our own. These children are beautiful, hard working, and well behaved. They know they are loved and wanted and are grateful to be receiving an education and a chance for a future. Although the government may decide to place some of them in foster care or arrange for local adoption, we plan to raise them until adulthood. They will always be part of our family.

In addition to my work with Compassion and Chantal's ministry with New Hope Home, we also became more involved in the community of the church in Rwanda. Although I was never a local pastor, I am an ordained Anglican priest. In Kigali, we became attached to St. Etienne Cathedral, where Chantal and I became very much involved and where I would often preach, participate in services, and teach pastors. Through St. Etienne (St. Stephen, as the name is known in English—the first deacon and a martyr of the early Christian Church), we also became active in fellowship outside the church.

Our activities through St. Etienne were, in many ways, a continuation of our ministry back in Charlottesville, Virginia, when we founded the Christian African Leadership Ministries (CALM) to provide training and resources for pastors. Now that we were in Kigali, we used our own resources and our connections in the evangelical Christian community to support local pastors with resources from bicycles to computers and to help establish vocational training centers to teach people useful skills, such as sewing. We also helped needy people, such as providing them with goats to elevate the living standard of rural farm families. We took to heart the old saying that if you give a person a fish, you feed him for a day; but teach that person to fish (or, in this case, how to sew or to raise goats), and you will feed him for his life. I can still remember one woman who was provided a goat and soon had a small herd of five; by selling one, she was able to afford the school fees to educate her children. Whenever we would meet, she would look at me so kindly and address me as "my son."

Separately and together, Chantal and I did whatever we could to make an impact in Rwanda. When the Rwandan cabinet asked me to serve as chairman of the School of Education, I was overjoyed. Moving back to Rwanda and contributing to the recovery and development of my country was deeply gratifying. I am so thankful that God provided me with so many different opportunities to contribute in many different roles.

In the five years since I returned to Africa, my ministry with Compassion had flourished. I had a job I loved and the personal satisfaction of helping to direct programs that changed the lives of so many children. But, as I saw in my life so many times, God sometimes interrupts the current trajectory of our lives with an unexpected course correction.

CHAPTER TEN

Becoming Bishop

". . . Whatever you have commanded us we will do,
and wherever you send us we will go . . ."
(Joshua 1:16b NIV)

For as long as I can remember, I wanted to be a minister. In my early days, growing up in the refugee camp in Burundi, I had been profoundly influenced by missionaries who came to care for us spiritually, emotionally, and physically. The only element I felt missing, which was so deeply desired and badly needed, was the economic empowerment of people to help themselves break the cycle of poverty—especially through education. Still, through the missionaries, I did experience God's loving care for all His children, especially the most vulnerable. These missionaries were early role models, pointing me in a direction by which I could attend to the vulnerable, the sick, the hurting, the lonely, and those who have lost their way.

As I have related thus far, my desire to pursue ministry took me in the direction of service through nonprofits, especially my eighteen years with Compassion International, where I found both a home and a deeply fulfilling purpose. As

Vice President for Program Development based in the Global Ministry Center in Colorado Springs, later moving to Africa, I was in a global leadership position that touched every aspect of my life: advocating for children, supporting the development of my home country of Rwanda, and contributing to the well-being of children and families in several countries across Africa. My work was rewarding, and my life felt complete. I was not looking for any major changes, other than to continue expanding Compassion's work on the African continent and providing leadership to my 450 staff members in eight African countries and two sub-regional offices (West & East Africa Area Offices).

Always aware of God's zigzag, into the comfort of my status quo came an unexpected calling. In 2009, a bishop in one of the dioceses of the Anglican Church of Rwanda told me he was retiring and a successor was being sought; he wondered if I could pray with him for his future replacement. He also suggested that I consider putting my name forward as a candidate. He confided that he and his wife had been praying for Chantal and me and were convinced that we were the people God was calling to the position. I had been ordained as an Anglican priest, and during our time in Kigali, I had become more active in ministry, including at St. Etienne where I was appointed to serve as a volunteer. I never saw myself pursuing church leadership. But the more I thought about it, the more I felt God was leading me to the next phase of my life of service—this time as a bishop of the Anglican Church, leading the Shyira Diocese in northwestern Rwanda. Encountering a call to serve as a church leader at this stage of my life involved many deep and complex parts. For one, my ministry with Compassion was flourishing; nothing was pulling me away from the work I loved. I had not the slightest inclination to look for something else (in fact, I would have been happy doing that work for many more years, all the way to my retirement). Not only was the work with Compassion extremely meaningful, it also enabled me to provide for my family.

However, I could not dismiss the idea of becoming a candidate for bishop—or, should I say, the idea would not dismiss me! And so, Chantal and I took it under prayerful consideration, meditating on the possibility that this was what God was leading me to do next. The more we prayed and discussed it, the more the idea made sense. Becoming bishop would bring another dimension to my ministry as a leader of the church, while putting my boots on the ground to work with pastors across the diocese and to elevate the people of Rwanda and beyond.

After several months of prayer, Chantal and I decided to allow my name to be submitted for consideration and election as a candidate bishop. I felt so many different and sometimes conflicting emotions. I was humbled by this opportunity and excited to apply the unique skill set I had developed throughout my career. At the same time, my being bishop would be a huge change for my family, especially financially. My family and I were comfortable and lived in a place where we felt secure. The more I reflected on this next phase of my life, the more the material aspects seemed to be the biggest stumbling block. Having grown up with virtually nothing and being poor as a young adult in Africa and as a college student in the U.S., it was easy for me to get by with modest means. But what of my children as they pursued their futures?

These conflicting desires and fears crystallized in a conversation I had with my daughter. We were sitting in Mimi's Café in Denver when Erica looked at me and said, "Daddy, the Lord will provide."

These were the same words I had spoken to my mother back in the refugee camp, when I was a hungry ten-year-old facing the possibility of starvation. I remember it like it was yesterday. How strong my conviction was as I went out into the jungle looking for something to eat. I can still hear the echo of my mother's bitter laugh of discouragement when I told her to boil water because I would find something. When I came back with that pumpkin, I knew without a doubt that I held one of God's countless small miracles in my hands.

Erica's comment brought me back to that moment of pure faith, the conviction that we do not need to know how, only that the Lord will provide. As a boy, in the midst of my hunger and desperation, it was relatively easy for me to believe. After all, my choices that day were either to put my trust in the Lord or to give up and die of starvation. But in the midst of my comfortable life, there were so many other considerations: a comfortable home, a lifestyle that enabled us to provide for our children (one finishing college, one a sophomore in college, and one pursuing his passion of film and acting), and the means to fund our charitable works, especially New Hope Homes. If elected bishop, I would be making only $500 a month, a tiny fraction of my Compassion income. I would be provided housing and utilities, plus a vehicle—if I could raise money for it.

Then my daughter asked me a pivotal question: "If you won the lottery today, Dad, and money wasn't the issue, would you do it?"

"Yes, of course, I would," I replied without hesitation.

"Then your worry is not about the call. You are thinking about us, your children, and how you are going to pay for our education and help support us. You have to trust, Dad. The Lord will provide."

While it was a little challenging to receive counseling from one of my children, it was a blessing, and I noted how wise and mature my daughter had become. Erica was not the only one who felt this way; all three of our children were willing to do whatever they could to support me should I become bishop. Erica assured me that she was willing to apply for student loans to finish her education. Eddie, the youngest, had a partial basketball scholarship to Eastern University, a private Christian college in Wayne, Pennsylvania. Eric could get a job while also pursuing acting. Although I had received prayers and counsel from many people during my time of discernment, Erica's perspective proved to be the most helpful as I wrestled with this calling. Without question, I knew that I could move forward into this new phase of life, with full support from Chantal and our children.

During this time, I also informed Compassion International that I was under consideration to become bishop. My colleagues were shocked, but also fully supportive as, once again, I made another step of faith into the unknown. They also recognized that this had happened before; indeed, my conviction to move to Rwanda had been so strong, I had been willing to leave Compassion to achieve that goal. Now, Chantal and I were embarking on what had become a familiar journey during which we would have to depend fully on the Lord's leading and His provision.

In December 2009, I received the news of my election as candidate bishop pending a final decision by the House of Bishops, which has responsibility for the final approval after the diocesan synod decision. I'll never forget where I was when I received the phone call: in the airport in Accra, Ghana, crossing the transit lounge to board my flight back to Kigali. The call came from one of the pastors who was in the synod that elected me. Then, in January 2010, the House of Bishops approved my election.

My consecration as bishop of Shyira Diocese was set for March 28, 2010, with my first official day of duties on Sunday, November 14, 2010. This gave me several months to prepare to hand over my duties at Compassion International.

The succession at Compassion brought home an important lesson about leadership: that each individual is part of continuum. A leader contributes to the organization within a specific time frame with a slate of particular responsibilities. Then it is the next person's time to step forward and contribute from his or her skill set and experiences. In this way, the organization continues to grow, with a dynamic pipeline of leaders at various stages of development. To me, good succession planning is the ultimate in servant leadership.

Before I left Compassion, my replacement, Sidney Muisyo, was named. (As of this writing, Sidney is Regional Vice President for Africa and has continued to expand Compassion's footprint on the continent.) Rather than a bureaucratic handover, the transition was marked with a ceremony held in June 2010 in Arusha, Tanzania, which gave me a wonderful sense of completion, while at the same time welcoming Sidney into his new role. This experience will forever stand as a hallmark for how leadership transitions can honor the succession process and highlight the contribution of everyone involved. If only more organizations today—for-profits, nonprofits, churches, and others—would follow this model.

Between June and October 2010, I met with church leaders and pastors as I began to get a more complete picture of the diocese and its current needs. On November 14 came the ceremony during which I was officially "seated" at the cathedral, with a complete handover of duties and responsibilities as Bishop of Shyira Diocese. My friend Dr. Charles Murigande, then Rwanda's Minister of Education, was the keynote speaker during a very colorful ceremony held on the grounds of the cathedral in Musanze. His speech brought back memories of our childhood and days in the refugee camp in Kigamba, Burundi.

Then came my consecration as bishop on March 28, a huge one-day celebration, attended by everyone: the local community, all the pastors, and church and even government leaders. President Kagame's speech still rings in my ears day as he emphasized the "importance of accountability among leaders . . . and the need to look after and care for the sheep."

The ceremony included traditional church music as well as Rwandan music and dancing. Prayers were offered, poetry was read, and Holy Communion was shared by all. Even though it rained all day, the heavy downpour lent its cadence to the music of the drums and the rhythm of the singing and speeches. It was as if heaven was blessing all of us. As Deuteronomy states, "The Lord will open the heavens, the storehouse of his bounty, to send rain on your land in season and to bless all the work of your hands" (Deut. 28:12 NIV).

How far I had come on this journey of faith, from a hungry, impoverished refugee to a church leader in the Anglican Church. Every step I had taken along my journey, from a poor, barefoot boy to becoming bishop, had led to this point. Like every phase of life, there have been (and continue to be) twists and turns, the unexpected opportunities and daunting challenges. I thought back on every one of them. The sustaining kindness of strangers along those 500 miles from Burundi to Kenya literally kept me going. There were bitter and even dangerous disappointments, such as being thrown in jail in Kenya because of mistaken identity and nearly being expelled from Bible college because I could not pay my tuition. At every juncture, the Lord was there, providing help, opening doors, and always putting someone on my path to help. But never in my wildest dreams had I ever imagined that I would serve Compassion International in a global leadership position or that I would become a bishop one day. Clearly the Lord was the author of the story of my life. I can only show my gratitude by being of service to others in the name of the Lord.

As bishop, my job was to oversee the Shyira Diocese. Located in the Musanze District, it measures about 200 square miles and has a population of approximately 370,000 people.

On my first official day as bishop, I was handed the symbolic crozier, which is a shepherd's crook or staff. This is a reminder that the bishop is the shepherd of God's flock. As we read in Isaiah: "He tends his flock like a shepherd: He gathers the lambs in his arms and carries them close to his heart; he gently leads those that have young" (Isaiah 40:11 NIV).

The next day, Monday, November 15, I went into the diocese office for the first time as bishop. Within moments, all the euphoria I had felt from my consecration and being seated as bishop popped like a balloon pierced with a pin. Almost immediately, I was hit by a notification from the bank, informing us that we were in default on a loan that had been taken out by the diocese to build a small hotel. We owed more than $1.2 million in principal, at today's dollar exchange rate, and unpaid accumulated interest. I sank into my chair in complete disbelief. I knew, of course, that the diocese had built a small hotel on the grounds near the cathedral in Musanze, with modest rooms that were sometimes used for church groups and retreats and also rented to travelers. What I did not know until that moment was that the hotel was not making any money and, therefore, did not generate enough cash to pay back the loan. Nowhere in the handover documents given to me was this loan mentioned, nor any of the financials for the hotel. The notification from the bank informed me that a bailiff would soon be dispatched to deliver foreclosure documents to seize the hotel. I needed to quickly negotiate with the bank to gain more time, while I investigated the problem and tried to find workable solutions.

The deeper I dug, the more I came to the sickening conclusion that my handover documents were not complete. The picture depicted was one of few assets and a lot of growth potential. The potential was there—all well-intentioned and spiritually driven to serve the people. The hotel, for example, had been built to provide jobs and to give a boost to the local community. But it became painfully clear to me that there had been no fiscal discipline to ensure that the growth could be sustained. Good intentions had led the diocese into an area—in this case, hospitality—where there was not sufficient expertise to overcome the challenges of operating a sustainable business.

My calling, the reason I had been elected bishop, now became clear in my own mind. I would spend the next year—from the end of 2010 through most of 2011—fixing the fiscal foundation. My primary concern was stabilizing the diocese's financing and paying down the growing debt, which was even larger than the $1.2 million owed on the hotel. As the challenges mounted, I also learned that the staff had not been paid for nine months. At the same time, I needed to develop a long-term plan to continue and expand in a sustainable way the good work that had taken root in the dioceses around community-building, education and opportunity, and evangelism.

Another challenge that I faced was the fact that I came from the NGO community without deep, long-term contacts in the diocese or throughout the church community. I did not have the benefit of relationships and networks across the Anglican/Episcopal church. Moreover, while the Shyira Diocese had enjoyed support from the West—including for the diocese's Sonrise Christian Boarding School, originally built to educate and house children orphaned during the genocide which today sees to the educational, physical, health, and spiritual needs of children, both those who are placed in the care of the diocese and those who are sent to the school by their families or other sponsors. I had not been introduced to these contacts. I felt like an outsider and needed to start building my own bridges of support for the diocese and for Sonrise.

As one challenge after another was revealed, it became clear that my transition to bishop was in stark contrast to what I had left behind at Compassion. But as the new leader of the diocese, I recognized that good succession planning could be one of my contributions. It would become my job to ensure the diocese's leadership pipeline was attended to, which meant identifying and developing those who had potential.

I will admit there were days I became so overwhelmed I wondered whether I could continue. The challenges were simply too many and too big. Then I would think back on the sense of calling I had experienced. Tackling these challenges brought me to my knees—literally. I prayed continually for guidance and discernment as I stepped into the unknown. The greater the problems, the greater my humility. I was more dependent than ever on the Lord.

I also recognized how I had been uniquely developed and positioned to take on this role. As I said in many speeches to donors and supporters at the time, "Yes, I am filling big shoes . . . but I am a size fourteen!"

For anyone facing challenges, whether personal or professional, do not let yourself become so overwhelmed by the problems that you fail to see how you have been prepared to find the right solution. Prior experiences yield lessons that help us to be creative when facing new problems. We recall how we handled difficulties in the past and we find the courage and inspiration to take on unexpected or unfamiliar challenges.

Fortunately, my eighteen years with Compassion had outfitted me with a very robust toolbox, particularly around education and program development, as well as management and leadership skills. As the depth and severity of the challenges in the diocese were revealed, it was time for me to open that toolbox—and open it wide. I also had to rely on help from others. For example, as I addressed fundraising within the diocese, I suggested pledge cards for members of the church; regular contributions of even modest amounts would help. A retired minister called me aside. "Bishop, this is too Western," he advised me. "People will consider it a strange approach." He explained that the traditional way was to pass a basket and ask all to contribute. If the amount collected was not enough the first time, the basket was passed again.

He was right, of course. People gave with a willing heart, even though it did not come anywhere close to the amount of money we needed for the diocese's operations. But at least we were able to ascertain the amount of money we could raise from the local congregations. I hoped to raise $500,000; the amount that came in was closer to $70,000. To supplement our finances, I made many trips abroad to speak to donors and to make new connections. Many of these people were generous not only in their financial support, but also in helping me to establish a broader network of connections to fund support for new programs and to shore up the diocese's financial foundation.

However, some of the sponsors in the United States and abroad, who had been so generous with the diocese and Sonrise School in particular, had been hurt by the 2007–08 financial crisis. When I took over the diocese in late 2010, some of these donors could not afford to be as generous as they had been in the past. Our new financial reality called for careful planning, budgeting, and execution, and I thanked God every day for my previous job experience, especially my time with Compassion.

We carried the financial problems for a while; however, paying down the debt was a priority. Working with the bank, we were able to forestall foreclosure, until we could sell the hotel property, which we did in June 2013. The hotel property was acquired by the police academy for dormitory housing. Our biggest financial problem was three large loans with interest rates ranging between 15 and 18 percent. A donor stepped up to pay them off, putting up about $475,000, and financed us at a much lower interest rate. The diocese paid him back slowly; then the donor forgave more than $62,000 in interest. Through the generosity of supporters, we were able to secure low- and no-interest loans that stabilized the diocese. For our part, the church had to commit to tight fiscal management: being careful in spending, never overextending ourselves, or initiating programs before we could sustain them financially.

Sonrise School was challenged by the fact that many of the students had no sponsors to pay their tuition. Some of those students didn't need sponsors—their families could pay their tuition)—but were listed as needing sponsorship. In order to improve the financial condition of the school, we had to make some significant changes in the school's management and the philosophy around sponsorship. We also needed to outsource some operations in order to save money.

Another challenge in the diocese was addressing the low-level of education and training among most of the pastors. Across the whole diocese only two pastors had a college education and two others held some level of diploma. The vast majority, though, had less than a ninth-grade education. What was discouraging at first soon became an opportunity: the development of a program to train pastors and thereby increase the level of leadership in the diocese. We started the Muhabura Biblical Study Center aimed at training pastors. Three levels of training were established: a certificate level, a diploma level, and a degree level. Each level holds sessions of two weeks per term (or six weeks per year for each level). As the training got underway, a few pastors were selected (and others continue to be selected) to pursue graduate degrees. As of this writing, six pastors have completed their master's degrees and more than 200 are enrolled in the different certificate, diploma, and degree levels.

Another aspect of training has been exposure trips to allow pastors to learn from other dioceses inside and outside Rwanda. Among the other initiatives I introduced was leadership retreats for pastors. We have used these retreats to identify and reflect upon our core values, such as love, truth, integrity, enthusiasm, and openness. Through songs, preaching, and liturgical messages, we have been able to put these values into action within the local congregations. As the diocese put greater emphasis on talent development, we undertook a much-needed challenge to ensure that we identify and develop emerging leaders. In addition, we are positioning our pastors to become community leaders and role models.

While the challenges have been considerable and much of the work is done behind the scenes, I can see why the Lord brought me into this position. Since becoming bishop, I have felt (and acted) like a CEO, a CFO, and an HR director. I have the organizational and management skills that have enabled me to fix the diocese's foundation, shoring up the finances and also addressing the talent needs. In addition, I have the skill of resilience, which has helped sustain me through some difficult challenges. But I never lost sight of the fact that I am a spiritual leader. And, I am sure, there have been some who expected me, because I am a bishop, not to be as much of a CFO when it came to budgeting and increasing accountability and transparency in our finances, but this, too, is part of doing God's work. Just as humans are complex with multiple dimensions, so are organizations—and especially the church.

Compartmentalizing is not as effective as taking on the whole. To me, this is the essence of a holistic ministry approach. In my role, I could not take on spiritual leadership and ignore the finances nor could I focus solely on the finances or succession planning and ignore spiritual development.

Within this holistic approach to ministry, I could secure a functioning and potentially thriving infrastructure as well as serving the needs of various communities while connecting them to God. In the midst of chaos, challenges, and questions, I was establishing something larger than myself, and doing it for a precious sector of the population that has always been my reason for being—the children. Once I was *of* the children, and now I could be *for* the children. It has always been about the children.

CHAPTER ELEVEN

Caring for the Children

*"So do not fear, for I am with you; do not be
dismayed, for I am your God. I will strengthen
you and help you; I will uphold you with my
righteous right hand." (Isaiah 41:10 NIV)*

As I confided in Chantal, my trusted advisor, the number of severe problems I had to address, she became as worried and frustrated as I. We tried not to say it to each other, but it was clear that each of us was wondering what we'd gotten ourselves into. The words of the Psalms captured the deep fears and worries we faced. "My soul is in deep anguish. How long, Lord, how long? Turn, Lord, and deliver me; save me because of your unfailing love" (Psalm 6:3-4 NIV). Yet Chantal and I clung to our belief that mine had been a true calling to this position, and that the Lord would show us the way.

One morning, I decided that instead of going into the diocesan office, I needed to spend a few hours clearing my head. When my mind was overly occupied, it was hard to "hear" the leading of the Lord. I reflected upon the prophet Elijah, who waited to experience the presence of the Lord on the mountain through a "great and powerful wind [that] tore the mountains apart and shattered the rocks"; through an earthquake and a fire. In the midst of all that tumult, Elijah did not experience God until he heard "a gentle whisper," and Elijah knew that was God (1 Kings 19:11-13 NIV). In the midst of my own equivalent of wind, earthquake, and fire, it was hard to discern my way forward; I needed calmness and quiet to receive spiritual guidance.

I suggested to Chantal that we take a drive, just the two of us. We had no destination in mind as we drove out of Musanze, which bustled with people going to market. These hard-working people, the lifeblood of the country, walked miles from the countryside to the city market to sell fruit and vegetables from their gardens.

Soon Musanze was behind us, and we headed out along rural roads through Rwanda's famous hills. In the distance were the Virunga Mountains, the old volcanoes called Karisimbi, Muhabura, Gahinga, Visoke, and Sabyinyo that rise as high as 4,500 meters (about 14,800 feet). The mountains are also home to the "silverback" mountain gorillas, made famous by the late zoologist Dian Fossey and the research center she had established to study these animals.

Thousands of tourists come to Rwanda each year for gorilla trekking. Led by guides, they ascend the mountains to see these beautiful creatures first hand. The tourism dollars are very important to Rwanda's economy and provide employment for porters, trackers, and guides, as well as in hotels and hospitality. The sad irony is that these expeditions to the Virguna Mountains travel along rural roads through some of the most entrenched poverty in Rwanda.

As Chantal and I drove along that morning, we passed through small villages and communities of one- and two-room houses made of mud brick, some with only a piece of cloth hanging in the front doorway. I could easily imagine that, even though Rwanda has achieved food security (meaning food shortages are no longer a widespread concern), people in places like this knew hunger. Subsistence farmers have only a small plot of land, often less than an acre, on which to grow crops to feed their family, sometimes with a little excess to sell. When you are poor, you never stop thinking about your next meal—where, how, and if you will get it.

Wherever we saw these clusters of small houses, we also saw children: two or three here, one by himself there. Sometimes, there would be a dozen under the age of five. When they spotted our car, they often ran toward the road, waving and shouting the way that children do, with no idea of who was driving by. Other times, they stood there—barefoot, wearing not much more than rags.

Just three or four years old, and sometimes younger, they were left to occupy themselves for hours at a time without adult supervision. The littlest were tended by siblings who were not much older than they; it was not uncommon to find a one-year-old toted on the hip of a five-year-old.

Children such as these are an all-too-common sight in poor rural areas around the globe. When parents have to work the fields so that the family can eat, children at very young ages are often left alone. It is not a case of neglect or abandonment, but necessity.

Chantal, with her mother's heart, began to worry out loud about the children. As a parent, I, too, worried. But the faces of these children tugged at my heart for another reason. I knew what it was like to stand by the side of a road, my stomach as empty as my pockets, and watch someone drive by. As a barefoot child in a refugee camp, I had run after the trucks that rolled in with food and supplies, but never enough to meet the needs of everyone. I remember picking up dried beans, one by one, that fell out of the sacks brought in on those trucks. A handful was a treasure.

"So many unattended children," I said to Chantal.

In Rwanda, as in much of Africa, most of the farmers are women. It is a common sight to see a woman with a baby wrapped in cloth on her back hoeing in the garden or picking crops. The men do odd jobs, gather firewood, and help transport the crops to market. With the adults occupied, the children are left by themselves. Vulnerable to becoming hurt, lost, or abused, these children were in need of loving care.

We could not be just another car driving by. These children were my responsibility, too. In my new role as bishop, I had to explore what the church could do to help them. We did not have much in the way of financial resources to provide for these children, but we did have a network of local parishes and willing people. We had to find a way.

Chantal and I returned to Musanze renewed and refreshed. In time, solutions to the diocese's pressing financial problems were found, often through the generosity and support of donors in the United States and Europe. One such donor is Tom Phillips, an American businessman and philanthropist, who never draws attention to himself. Spiritually motivated, Tom is a social entrepreneur who acts only out of his desire to honor God through service to others. On one of Tom's many visits to Rwanda, I asked him if he would accompany me on a drive. The two of us headed to Gisenyi on the shores of Lake Kivu, bordering the Democratic Republic of the Congo (DRC). On that ride to Gisenyi, I poured out my heart to Tom, especially my desire to attend to the needs of the children. I did not want to burden Tom, but thought of him as my brother in the Lord. As we sat together on the shores of Lake Kivu, which is a huge body of water, I thought of the Sea of Galilee where Jesus called his first disciples, starting with two brothers, Simon (kater called Peter) and Andrew. "They were casting a net into the lake, for they were fishermen. 'Come, follow me,' Jesus said, 'and I will send you out to fish for people.' At once they left their nets and followed him" (Matthew 4:18-19 NIV). Now Tom and I were discerning what we were called to do to help the children.

A plan unfolded: Shyira Diocese has a network of 335 local parishes (and still growing). The church building where people gather on Sunday is empty the rest of the week. These buildings (often very modest structures) could be used for preschools, open to all children in the community, regardless of their religious affiliation. As a holistic solution, from playing to praying to learning, the preschools would be a child protection solution, a safe place for these youngsters to spend the morning hours while their mothers worked the fields. And, because the women could work the fields without worrying about their children, the preschools would also be a poverty-alleviation solution.

When the idea was presented to pastors in the diocese, four became "early adopters" to test the idea. Six months later, in mid-2011, we had sixteen preschools. Now, as of this writing, we have 217 preschools, serving more than 22,000 children, age three to six. These "early childhood education centers," as we call them, are probably more modest than what comes to mind when you say preschool in more developed countries. In our centers, you won't find brightly lit classrooms or playgrounds with slides, swings, and climbing bars. More important than the furnishings is the safety and loving care provided to the children in their local communities.

The preschools are staffed by teachers who are trained by the diocese; they teach in both Kinyarwanda and English, giving the children an early introduction to bilingual skills that will serve them well later in life. It is a beautiful sight to see, early in the morning, the children being led by the hand by their parents to school—clean, happy, and ready to learn. Our goal is for each local congregation to have a preschool. We actually have been able to influence other churches in Rwanda and outside the country, such as in Zambia, to start church based and sustainable pre-primary centers.

In a growing number of the diocesan preschools, the diocese partners with One Egg, a nonprofit organization (www. oneegg.org) that provides locally sourced eggs to children. One Egg started in Rwanda out of a conversation I had with Tom Phillips. Its mission to improve the nutrition and development of children in rural areas was quickly supported by Tyson Foods. Since then One Egg's operations have expanded from Rwanda, to Haiti, Uganda, Mozambique, Zimbabwe, Honduras, and Nicaragua, and continues to grow.

The eggs, delivered fresh from a local farm, can be kept at room temperature with ample shelf life, making them a portable and convenient protein source. In the late morning, the eggs are hard-boiled over a wood fire and then distributed to the children. Watching the children—often as many as a hundred in each preschool—at "egg time" is a joyful experience. First they line up to wash and rinse their hands (which helps reinforce basic hygiene habits), then they say grace, and then the eggs are distributed by the adults to the children. No one eats until all are served. Even the peeling is quite orderly, and little ones who struggle with the hard shells are helped by the older children.

While we would, ideally, love to have eggs made available to all our preschool children, we can only do so where there is sponsorship. But the preschoolers who do not receive eggs are nurtured in many other ways. The children are safe and secure; they have opportunities to learn and socialize, stimulating the development of their bodies and their brains. From this young age, they start out on a path toward education and self-empowerment.

We know that children who are nurtured and cared for have a better chance to be healthy, and develop thinking, language, emotional, and social skills that help them achieve their full potential as adults. In Rwanda, according to a UNICEF report, only about 12 percent of children between three and six have access to early learning and development, and most of those services tend to be in urban areas and too costly for poorer parents. The need for holistic and integrated early childhood development services are the greatest among poor and vulnerable families.*

At the risk of boasting about our program, it seems that the Shyira Diocese is doing exactly what needs to be done to promote early childhood development in a rural area where the need is so great. Like parents everywhere, the people of Shyira Diocese want their children to thrive; providing a future for the next generation is a universal motivation. I often encounter parents in the diocese who are enthusiastic toward their preschool children learning. One father could not be prouder. "He can speak English!" he told me excitedly.

---

*Unicef.org, Rwanda, Early Childhood Development, www.unicef.org/rwanda/education_8301.html

Although we have not officially measured school readiness among our preschoolers, we have anecdotal evidence that participation in our early childhood program gives these children an advantage when they enter school. Not only have many grasped the basics of math and literacy, they also know how to behave in a group-learning environment.

Within the communities the difference is visible between children who attend preschools and those who do not. Often this encourages more parents to send their children to the preschools. (And, as a fringe benefit, the preschools support a sense of community and help build church membership, too!) As we expand the early childhood program, one issue is always sustainability. To fund the preschools, we've had to get creative—keeping the program affordable while having the parents offset the cost of running the preschools. Parents pay 500 Rwandan francs (about 70 cents) per month, or the equivalent of a half day of manual work, to send their child to the program. Most can afford such a small amount. (The average per capita income in Rwanda has been on the rise, currently about $1,000 per year.) Those who have no money can pay for preschool tuition by working for the church; for example, in the pastor's garden.

As our preschools grow, the idea is catching on. Within Rwanda, more churches are taking note of what we've done in Shyira Diocese. By replicating what we've done, more churches can offer early childhood education in their communities to serve the needs of children and families across the country. Word about our programs also has spread outside Rwanda. An archbishop in Zambia heard about our program and sent five of his pastors to spend a week with us. In August 2015, with support from Compassion International, a team from Shyira Diocese and a Compassion staff member made a follow-up visit to Zambia to cast a broader vision of child advocacy among seventy-five pastors and one bishop. While in Zambia, we were pleased to learn that four of the pastors who had previously visited us already started programs in their parishes.

While the preschools remain a priority, the diocese is also active on the other end of the educational spectrum with a vocational school located in Musanze. My predecessor had advocated for a university to be built, but that was beyond our means and capabilities. However, the idea morphed into a vocational school. This was not only more doable for us, but also provides valuable training in practical skills—welding, construction, computer science, hospitality and hotel management, and electrical, among others—to help people get a job. The idea of a polytechnic/community college caught on, and as of this writing we have 900 students enrolled. As we roll out our next phase, we are developing business incubators to give students practical experience and to help offset the cost of running the school. Our first business was making and selling bricks, and then using those bricks to do construction. Other business opportunities at the school include catering; we have a small restaurant with a full-sized kitchen, and we have hosted weddings on the grounds.

The diocese's other services today include a health center and 694 "savings groups" created to empower people economically and to foster a culture of saving. Our Mother's Union, a women's ministry, runs economic empowerment programs designed to teach widowed and HIV-positive women marketable skills.

"Business for mission" (just as Chantal and I had done back in the States to support pastor training in Africa) is a tangible way to "feed" people in diverse ways: through education, training, employment, and other opportunities. For example, in 2015, the diocese recently opened a small, twenty-three-room hotel, The Garden Place Hotel. As of the end of the year, we have been averaging 60 percent occupancy, earning money that has allowed us to service our loan commitment to a donor who provided financing. We believe that we will be able to pay back this debt and, when we do, the hotel will generate a significant amount of money to support diocesan operations, including for training pastors at our Muhabura Bible Center. As of this writing in late 2016, our donor has challenged us that if we can raise $150,000 to pay off the hotel debt, he will forgive the other $50,000.

Another social entrepreneurship venture is the Nova Complex, a commercial building that was financed with grants and loans (thanks to a loyal supporter, Drayton Nabers) which have since been off. The space is open to any reputable business; our current tenants include an airline office, pharmacy, bank, and small grocery store.

On the financial side, we have identified a need among the people of the diocese to be able to access savings and loans programs and for financial education. The diocese has also created a small revolving fund designed to make modest amounts of capital available to people to help lift them out of poverty, for example by helping them start a small business or increase the production on their farms.

We also developed a retirement plan for pastors and diocesan staff, the first of its kind. Until this time, social security fund contributions had been made by the diocese only for office personnel. The pastors, however, were not provided for in retirement. Today, the diocese has a pension plan in place. Parishes contribute to the plan for their pastors, with contributions ranging from 1,000 to 2,000 Rwandan francs

($1.40 to $2.80) per month, depending on the capacity the parish. Now, pastors have the peace of mind that, when the time comes to retire, they will receive a stipend based on the number of years in service. Before, retirement meant only receiving one or two sheets of corrugated metal for his roof, and a bicycle or a cow—and sometimes only two of the three.

As these initiatives show, social entrepreneurship and business for mission are the job of the church. The diocese needs to contribute to the well-being and development of the people, enabling them to build better lives for themselves and their families. It is the church's work to raise people up and give them hope, to help them find a way to use their God-given gifts and talents to support themselves and contribute to their communities. And, as their incomes improve, they likely will help support the diocese and its efforts to minister to others. If the church does nothing, people become demoralized, leading to a downward cycle of continued poverty and disempowerment that makes people dependent on the church and others for handouts and support. An integrated solution including social entrepreneurship lead to more sustainable programs for the diocese—and self-sustainability for individuals.

Yes, we need to generate more capital and develop our human resources to get where we need to be. But we are encouraged by our progress thus far. Given where were started, deeply in debt and with a decline in donor support because of the global financial crisis, we have made great progress.

My role as bishop has evolved, from fixing problems and launching initiatives, to the next phase: sustainability. In the past, churches in developing economies such as Rwanda depended heavily on funding from the West. In recent years, that funding source has diminished. For one, there is donor fatigue. In addition, church demographics in the West are changing; the membership base is aging and is not being replaced in the same numbers by the younger generation. At the same time, the church in the global south is growing, in membership and vibrancy. In order for the church in Africa to be strong, it needs to be self-funding, which increases the importance of initiatives such as business for missions. In Shyira Diocese, we hope to achieve sustainability for our programs within five years, as of this writing.

As we talk to people in the diocese about the importance of self-sufficiency, we are blessed to have a role model in our government leaders, who stress the importance of self-reliance and self-sufficiency for the country. On the local level, the church can advance this thinking, showing people how to become self-sustaining and self-directed. Together, we can do for ourselves, knowing that the Lord will provide.

In my life today, I am blessed with another important part of my life of service: Compassion International. Although I left Compassion to enter ministry with the church, my relationship with this wonderful organization has continued. In fact, when I left, Compassion's president, Wess Stafford, told me that if I ever wanted to come back, the door would always be open to me. I also told my Compassion colleagues that if they ever needed anything from me, they should just ask.

In October 2010, I saw Wess Stafford in Capetown, South Africa, at the Lausanne Movement on World Evangelization. He approached me with an interesting opportunity: Compassion wanted to have board members with experience as global staff and who represented the countries served. I had both, which Wess felt would make a significant contribution to Compassion's leadership.

I was so honored that Compassion would consider me for board membership, and eagerly agreed to pursue this opportunity. I saw the win–win potential of contributing my knowledge and experience to an organization I greatly admired, while also gaining perspective and ideas that might help the diocese. (The fact that I could also see my children in the States when I went back for Compassion board meetings was also a plus.)

As I went through the process of joining the Compassion board, Chantal and I were invited to attend a meeting in Indonesia. I attended as a general member, with no voting rights. Everything was going along well until we discovered a conflict of interest: our daughter, Erica, worked for Compassion in Colorado. I did not want my daughter to lose her job, but when we discussed the situation as a family, she quickly spoke up. "Dad, I can find another job," she told me. "If Compassion really wants you, I would like to see you join the board."

I went back to the board and told them Erica was willing to find another job, which opened the way for me to become a full board member. Erica is now working in Rwanda, a move that she made after much soul-searching. Every time she thought about the possibility, a million excuses came to her mind of why this wasn't the right time. She admitted that the delay in making a decision was due to fear. As she put it, "Fear of the unknown . . . not knowing what I would do in Rwanda. I didn't know how I would fit in or if I would be accepted in the culture. I didn't know if I could find friends and a church community like the one I loved in the U.S."

Erica later shared that her decision to move to Rwanda was sparked by the example of what the Lord had done in my life. She told me, "I started to think about the many times you made the touch decisions to walk by faith because deep down in your heart, there was a stirring from the Lord. It didn't make the actions easy, nor did it make the doubts and worries go away, but I felt the peace of God that said, 'Go, and I will be with you. Do not fear.'"

For any parent—indeed, for any person—one of the greatest satisfactions is knowing that we have helped others by being an example of trust. There is no ego involved, no desire to make a point about "doing it my way." On the contrary, it is the example of surrender, in spite of the doubts and fear. If there is any message I hope readers will carry away from this book, it is that. Trust. Have faith. Know that you are never alone or forgotten. The Lord will provide.

In my life, with perspective that develops with time and distance from an event, I came to see that doors do not close without a reason. Perhaps, as the saying goes, God is about to open a window somewhere else. Or, the disappointment builds our resilience as we test our resolve. Sometimes it is a matter of timing as the pieces to come together. Whatever the reason, our lives never follow a straight line. God's path is always a zigzag, and in every corner or U-turn there is a lesson. Often, we can't see it or fully appreciate it until we look back, in retrospect. In order to learn these lessons, though, we have to be proactive about them, meditating on the circumstances and events, even years later. *What did I learn? What do I know about myself and others now that I did not know before? Where did I experience the unconditional love of God in the unexpected kindness and generosity of strangers? How did certain events change me? How did others' treatment of me influence how I treat others?*

❧

As of this writing, I have served for four years on the board of Compassion International, including as vice chairman. In addition to serving on the board nomination and board development committees, my role has brought multiple perspectives based on all my experiences, from global staff and field office, to the person being served. Given that Compassion partners with churches in the field, I have also brought the perspective of a church leader.

In the next 16 months, the time will come for me to exit my current role as bishop; then another will take over. My successor is Bishop Sam Mugisha, who was consecrated on March 5, 2017, and is serving as coadjutor bishop. I always knew this transition would not lead to retirement and sitting in a rocking chair. Rather, it would be a time to change activities, continuing my passion and mission to serve others, wherever God would send me.

In my heart, I feel that Africa will always be a focus of my life and work, but also beyond. Through my life and experiences, I have become a global person. Our family, too, is global; Erica lives in Rwanda now, and Eric and Eddie are in the United States. We have learned to love where we are, but never become so attached to one place that we isolate or limit ourselves in any way. For example, when we bought our two-and-a-half acres to build our dream home in Colorado, Chantal and I prayed that we would not put down roots too deep. When we heard the Lord's next calling, we did not want to struggle or not respond. As we built our home, we prayed to be ready to leave it when that time came.

Now, Chantal and I have a beautiful home in Musanze, and open our doors to visitors from the United States, Europe, and Africa. But if God called me tomorrow to China or Brazil, or anywhere else on this planet, I would go. With the toolbox the Lord has given me, there are many places I could go and be of service because of who I am, where I have been, what I believe, and with all that God has blessed me.

I am open to God's leading. He has taken me farther in life than I ever thought possible, from a barefoot refuge boy, to executive of a global organization, to bishop. There have been challenges along the way, and no doubt will be more. But from the jungle of Burundi where a pumpkin appeared, to a long walk to Kenya, across college campuses in the U.S., and throughout my career, I know one thing without a doubt: The Lord will provide.

May the Lord make your love increase and overflow
for each other and for everyone else . . .
(1 Thessalonians 3:12)

Pursuing the Windows of Faith

". . . my heart is glad and my tongue rejoices; my body will rest secure . . ." (Psalm 16:9 NIV)

If there is one thing I have learned in my life, it is not to give up—and definitely not to do so too soon.

I add this last phrase because it is often the difference between fulfillment and disappointment. Worse than giving up—and sometimes we do need to alter course and take up a new plan—is that people do it too soon. When faced with initial defeat, it is so easy to give up. All the evidence appears in that moment to refute your hope and revile your dream. Faith is what keeps you going beyond that first defeat, believing that there is still reason to hope. Your eyes remain open for detours and side routes that take you in unexpected, but ultimately more satisfying, directions. If you give up quickly, though, you never get far enough down the path to see where you might have gone. If you stop moving forward and decide that the status quo is the best you can hope for, you give up on yourself. Then you are truly defeated.

When I look back on my life—surviving in the refugee settlement as a child, the long walk to Kenya, my trials and disappointments in my early career, and constant money worries while getting my doctorate—I wonder what would have happened if I had given up the first time things became difficult. Where would I be now? Would the purpose God intended in my life, as God does in everyone's life, have been fulfilled? These questions lead me to one answer and that is the sustaining power of grace, to fill in the gaps when human courage, endurance, and willpower begin to falter. When we hit a dead end, grace signals the turn up ahead—the one we can only see if we continue moving.

I call this pursuing the window. A well-known expression is that when God closes a door, He opens a window. While I know this to be true, I would argue that this old saying does not go quite far enough. The leap of faith is knowing that God will open a window and pursuing that window even when you don't see it. When the door closes, you step out in faith that the window, which may be hidden from your view at first, is there. As Paul wrote to the Corinthians: "For we live by faith, not by sight" (2 Cor 5:7 NIV).

Keep moving forward until the window is apparent. And if that window ends up being another closed door, then you pursue the next window and the next. This is the zigzag walk of faith that I've talked about earlier, the twists and turns that build faith and fortitude. Oh, that any of us would be able to walk a straight line through life—how much easier that would be! But what lessons and opportunities to build our faith we would miss that then become an example and inspiration to others.

So how do we know when the window appears? We can tell by our past experiences. When we contemplate previous attempts that were not initially successful or ways we found to move forward in a similar situation, we discover clues of where and how to look for windows. We see patterns in our lives—some inspirational and some tactical. It may be that talking with a mentor helped you figure out a better approach or spending time with family and friends enabled you to ask for help or to receive resources that were there for the asking.

God's unexpected windows come in all shapes and sizes. It may be a person who taps you on the shoulder and says, "I have another idea for you." It may be something you see or read that inspires you to move in a new direction. You will find the windows to pursue if you keep moving, asking for help, and knowing that you are not alone.

And, as a person of faith, I would tell you that prayer works. My spiritual life as a Christian has been marked by moments of absolute certainty that the Lord was at my side in the most difficult and trying circumstances. In that jail in Kenya, when I had given up all hope of not only not reaching my dream but even of living for another day, the Lord provided for me. Who else could have whispered into the ear of the head mistress of the college, making her realize that I was not the man she feared?

We learn from the past, but we must not become prisoner to it. The old has no hold on us when we keep moving forward toward new windows; in the process, we, too, are made new. One of my favorite quotes, which always inspires me, is from Paul's message to the Corinthians: "Therefore, if anyone is in Christ, the new creation has come. The old has gone, the new is here!" (2 Cor 5:17 NIV).

As a new creation, you become a beacon of hope for others. Your personal knowledge of difficulties and disappointments, your experiences wrestling with self-doubt and despair, can be put to good use in the lives of others. Your wounds are the source of your compassion for others. I do not think I would have been as passionate about my ministry or my work with Compassion International had I not lived the life I did, particularly when I was young and faced so many challenges. Having known poverty and hunger, I can look into the eyes of a child in need and know the joy and the obligation to provide help.

The harshest shackle on human potential is poverty. When you have nothing, it is so easy to become engulfed by the negatives that limit your worldview: *I am poor, and I always will be poor.* It takes tremendous faith and hope to break the cycle of poverty. The greatest gift, therefore, especially for children born into poverty, is education. Education is anything that contributes to learning and expansion of human potential. If that includes secondary education and college one day, then praise the Lord! But it starts with opening children's minds to learning, to acquiring skills, and to gaining a body of knowledge about themselves and the world. With even a modest education, they can see themselves as capable and resourceful, so that they, too, can pursue the "windows" that God has for them.

Sometimes people ask me, "What can I do? The problems of the world are so big and I'm just one person—and I'm not a millionaire!"

My response is to do something. If you feel compelled to help the children of Africa, then find a small way to do it, such as through an organization dedicated to improving the lives of these children. If you are compelled to support people in other circumstances, whether in your community or your own country, those whose lives are limited by illiteracy, poverty, or a lack of opportunity, then do that. Trust that as you move forward in your life of giving, windows will appear there, too.

Wherever you are and whatever your means, look for ways to open the door for someone else. It does not have to be material or monetary. It can be a few words of encouragement. Never will I forget the woman in Kenya who gave me, at the time a ragged young man with no idea where my next meal was coming from, an ear of roasted corn and seventeen shillings for the bus. She made all the difference in my life that day.

Because of her help and her example, I have been inspired to look for opportunities to uplift others and make a difference in their lives. Following her example, you, too, can start with where you are and what you have to share. You will make a far bigger impact than you can imagine. The life you touch and transform today will touch another life tomorrow. As we say in Compassion International, "One life at a time." Suddenly, an entire community begins to change. If we want to change the world, it begins right where we are.

Happiness does not come from earthly things. Our joy is rooted in relationships and community. Find your community and become part of it. If you do not see a community, then create one. When you belong, you will become uplifted and able to uplift others.

Finally, trust that what you need will be provided to you. It may not be exactly what you want or think you want. But you will not be abandoned. As a young boy, weak from hunger and with no food to eat, I told my mother to boil water because "the Lord will provide."

What if I had not gone out in the jungle that day? What if I had given up? Would my family and I have died of starvation as others in the refugee settlement did?

Surely there was no reason to believe that day would be any different from the others. The "door" to what normally would have saved us had closed; no relief supplies came that day or during the ones before. Instead, I pursued the only window I could imagine. I wandered into the jungle, believing with all my heart that I would come back with something. Every time a hunger pain twisted my stomach, I repeated encouraging words to myself: "The Lord will provide." You know the rest of the story: I found a pumpkin—the first of many such fruits of faith from the Lord.

And, I pray, it will be the same for you on your path through life, through twists and turns, beyond closed doors to the windows of opportunity that you pursue.

About the Author

The Rt. Rev. Dr. Laurent Mbanda was born in Rwanda and spent his childhood years in Burundi; he has since lived in many countries. Today he serves as the Bishop of Shyira Diocese in the Anglican Church of Rwanda.

Bishop Mbanda joined the Compassion International family in 1993 as program director for Africa, and he has since held several different positions in the ministry, including Vice President of Africa Region.

In 1994, during and immediately following the genocide in Rwanda, Bishop Mbanda was asked to serve as relief manager in Rwanda, rescuing children, providing relief to all who needed assistance, and establishing rehabilitation and development programs in the aftermath of this human tragedy. Mbanda then moved to the United States as a program development specialist, and in June 1996 was promoted to executive director of program development, a global position in which he oversaw Compassion's involvement in twenty-three countries. In 1997, he became vice president of program development, also a global position, and served on the organization's executive leadership team.

Mbanda later served as Compassion International's associate director for Africa, with responsibility for an HIV/AIDS curriculum, and in 2005 became Africa director for Compassion, and then vice president for Africa in 2006.

In March 2010, Mbanda was consecrated Bishop of Shyira Diocese in Rwanda's Northern Province, overseeing more than three hundred local Anglican congregations. He is a member of the board of Compassion International and has been vice chairman of the board since 2012.

Mbanda is also a board member and chair of Food for the Hungry Associates, based in Phoenix, Arizona, and a board member of the International Justice Mission, based in Washington, DC. He previously served as chairman of the board of the Kigali Institute of Education, appointed by the Rwandan government.

He was ordained as an Anglican priest in 1988.

Prior to joining Compassion International, Bishop Mbanda was Africa director for Christian Aid Mission in Charlottesville, Virginia, and was country director for Burundi with Campus Crusade.

Mbanda is a graduate of Kenya Highlands Bible College and has completed coursework for his M.A. in Missiology from Fuller Seminary's School of World Missions. He also holds an M.A. in Christian Education from Denver Seminary and a Ph.D. from Trinity International University in Deerfield, Illinois. He is fluent in English, French, Swahili, and several other African languages.

He and his wife, Chantal, reside in Musanze, Rwanda. They have three grown children (Erica, Eric, and Edwin), and have cared for another twenty-eight Rwandan children for the past nine years.

Genocide destruction in Rwanda.

Relief supplies for Rwanda.

Bishop Mbanda at this graduation with
his dear wife, Chantal, and Ruth Mackellen.

Bishop Mbanda's family. From left to right:
Erica, Edwin, Laurent, Chantal, and Eric.

Bishop Mbanda with Ph.D. dissertation advisor
and professor Dr. Ted Ward.

Bishop Mbanda (2nd from left); next is his great
uncle, Petero Sebaheka, and his family.

Rev. Vincent Strigas (left) and Bishop Mbanda, interpreting.
(Rev. Strigas was like a father to me! He inspired me
for graduate work.)

Erica (left) and Eric, amazed by the baby cow at
Bishop Mbanda's childhood refugee resettlement
(Kigamba refugee settlement).

Bishop Mbanda at mass in St. Trinity Cathedral, receiving communion following his ordination as deacon in the Anglican Church of Burundi by Archbishop Samuel Sindamuka (far right). Left is Rev. Norman and to the right, Rev. Naniye.

Rev. Dr. Laurent Mbanda in his Diocesan Office in Musanze, Rwanda.

Looking over curriculum materials in Quito, Peru,
with my former colleagues Jose Carrasco (center)
and Mark Yeadon (right).

In Lima, Peru, with Enrique Pinedo and Doug Basset
(toward the rear).

Bishop Mbanda and guests in Africa.

Cheetahs at the Nairobi animal rescue
(from left) Erica and Eric.